# Creating a Sens... Immigrant and Refugee Students

Discover how to create a sense of belonging and connection for your immigrant and refugee students. This timely book, written by four award-winning teachers, offers compelling stories and practical applications to help you reach your students in the classroom and beyond.

Topics covered include advocacy, using literacy to create a welcoming environment, connecting with families, building staff capacity and best practices for virtual learning. You'll also find easy-to-implement lesson plans, as well as reflection questions throughout to help you on your journey.

Appropriate for K-12 teachers, English Learner specialists and school leaders, this inspiring and useful book will help you make the necessary changes to create more positive outcomes for your immigrant students.

**Mandy Manning** recently transitioned from a 21-year career as a classroom teacher, to advocating for educators, public schools and students as the Digital Content Specialist for the Washington Education Association. For the previous 8 years Mandy was the first teacher for newly arrived refugee and immigrant students at Ferris High School in the Newcomer Center in Spokane, WA. Mandy is the 2018 National Teacher of the Year.

**Ivonne Orozco Sahi** teaches high school Spanish in Albuquerque. As a first-generation college student, immigrant, former DACA recipient, queer woman of color, Ivonne has found her voice in education through her intersectionalities. Ivonne is a co-founder of Teachers Against Child Detention and is the 2018 New Mexico Teacher of the Year.

**Leah Juelke**, the 2018 North Dakota Teacher of the Year, is a high school English Language Arts teacher, K-12 English Learner specialist and literacy coach in Fargo, North Dakota. She is a decorated educator whose passion for global education, literacy and creating a welcoming community for refugee and immigrant English Learners earned her a spot as one of the top 10 teachers in the world and a finalist for the Global Teacher Prize in 2020.

**Sarahí Monterrey** is an English Learner teacher at Waukesha South School. She was named Wisconsin's 2018–2019 High School Teacher of the year. She was selected as Wisconsin's 2019 State Teacher of the Year representative to the National Teacher of the Year program and is the first Latina in the state of Wisconsin to have this honor. As a child immigrant from El Salvador, Sarahí Monterrey recognizes the pivotal role teachers play in students' lives.

# Creating a Sense of Belonging for Immigrant and Refugee Students

## Strategies for K-12 Educators

Mandy Manning, Ivonne Orozco Sahi,
Leah Juelke and Sarahí Monterrey

Routledge
Taylor & Francis Group

NEW YORK AND LONDON

Cover image: © Getty Images

First published 2022
by Routledge
605 Third Avenue, New York, NY 10158

and by Routledge
2 Park Square, Milton Park, Abingdon, Oxon, OX14 4RN

*Routledge is an imprint of the Taylor & Francis Group, an Informa business*

*Library of Congress Cataloging-in-Publication Data*
A catalog record for this title has been requested

ISBN: 978-1-032-01140-0 (hbk)
ISBN: 978-1-032-00008-4 (pbk)
ISBN: 978-1-003-17733-3 (ebk)

DOI: 10.4324/9781003177333

Typeset in Palatino LT Std
by KnowledgeWorks Global Ltd.

To all immigrant and refugee students who
are tremendous gifts to this nation.

# Contents

# Meet the Authors

**Mandy Manning** recently transitioned from a 21-year career as a classroom teacher, to advocating for educators, public schools and students as the Digital Content Specialist for the Washington Education Association. For the previous 8 years Mandy was the first teacher for newly arrived refugee and immigrant students at Ferris High School in the Newcomer Center in Spokane, WA. Mandy is the 2018 National Teacher of the Year. With 2018 New Mexico Teacher of the Year, Ivonne Orozco Sahi, Mandy co-founded Teachers Against Child Detention, urging educators to act on behalf of immigrant children incarcerated across the U.S. and denied their right to education and freedom. She lives in Spokane, Washington.

**Ivonne Orozco Sahi** is the 2018 New Mexico Teacher of the Year. Ivonne was born and raised in Chihuahua, Mexico until she was 12 years old when her family immigrated to the United States. She learned English through middle school and graduated high school in central New Mexico. It was during these challenging years of learning that Ivonne was encouraged by her teachers to grow. Ivonne knows the power that educators hold to create positive change in students' perspectives of themselves.

Ivonne attended the University of New Mexico where she earned her B.A. and M.A. in Secondary Education. She teaches high school Spanish in Albuquerque, NM. Ivonne creates interactive, challenging lessons with real-world connections for all students regardless of language background. Her culturally sustaining pedagogy operates on student strengths and values the contributions of all. As a first-generation college student, immigrant, former DACA recipient, queer, woman of color, Ivonne has found her voice in education through her intersectionalities. Ivonne is a co-founder of Teachers Against Child Detention a national and local movement that advocates for the rights of the immigrant community.

**Leah Juelke**, the 2018 North Dakota Teacher of the Year, is a high school English Language Arts teacher, K-12 English Learner specialist and literacy coach in Fargo, North Dakota. She is a decorated educator whose passion for global education, literacy and creating a welcoming community for refugee and immigrant English Learners earned her a spot as one of the top 10 teachers in the world and a finalist for the Global Teacher Prize in 2020. Leah is a certified teacher and holds a Bachelor's degree in English Education and EL, a Master's degree in Curriculum and Instruction, and has started work on her Ph.D. in Reading, Literacy and Assessment. Throughout her career, she has taught in and/or traveled to over 27 different countries. Her teaching experience includes working with students of all grade levels within private, charter and public schools.

When Leah is not coaching debate and student congress, she enjoys spending time with her two children, Samara and Salazander. As a National Geographic Certified Educator, Leah collaborates with classrooms around the globe and strives to create "a classroom without borders" that breeds empathy, engagement and empowerment. Through her Journey to America, Green Card Voices and We Are America literacy projects, Leah helps to amplify the voices of her refugee and immigrant students and empowers them to advocate for social justice.

As a child immigrant from El Salvador, **Sarahí Monterrey** recognizes the pivotal role teachers play in students' lives. Sarahí's approach to teaching embodies a genuine belief that every student has the ability to learn and grow, and every educator has an obligation to tear down the barriers that stand in students' way. Sarahí has been teaching in the School District of Waukesha for the past 14 years of her 19-year teaching career. She is currently an English Learner teacher at Waukesha South School. Sarahí was named Wisconsin's 2018–2019 High School Teacher of the year. She was selected as Wisconsin's 2019 State Teacher of the Year representative to the National Teacher of the Year program and is the first Latina in the state of Wisconsin to have this honor.

# Acknowledgements

First and foremost, I want to thank my students. It is you who inspired the work within these pages and my strong desire to ensure that every environment is welcoming and recognizes the gifts you bring to our nation and communities. I also want to thank Lauren Davis for believing in this project and the incredible team at Routledge for bringing this book to life. A huge thank you and tremendous love to Ivonne, Leah and Sarahí for your dedication to this project and for being such incredible educators, advocates and friends. Finally, thank you to my incredible family, Katie, Ryan, Hussein, Bailey, Faith, Harper and my mom, Kathy, for supporting me and loving me unconditionally. I couldn't do anything in this life without all of you.

**–Mandy Manning**

Quiero dar gracias a mis padres que fueron los primeros soñadores, y a mis hermanas que siempre me echan porras: gracias por su apoyo. I'd also like to thank my wonderful wife, Nadia Orozco-Sahi, for ensuring that through the growth of our family we were also growing professionally and supporting each other, I could not do anything that I do without your love. I am grateful to all of my teachers and professors who have always believed in my potential and let me know through actions or words, I only wish to embody every single one of you every day. A big thanks to Mandy, Leah and Sarahí, who made this beautiful project a possibility and reality. And finally, I would like to thank my students: Gracias, I learn from you more than you know.

**–Ivonne Orozco Sahi**

It really does take a village. The work that I do every day in the classroom is a collaborative effort, and this book is no different. It could not have been written without the collaboration of my dedicated and accomplished co-authors; Mandy, Sarahí and Ivonne. The writing process is never easy, even for this English teacher, but with our amazing publisher, Lauren Davis and the Routledge/Taylor & Francis Group, the process was seamless and organized.

In addition, I am greatly appreciative of the 2018 class of State Teachers of the Year (STOY) and all the amazing educators that I have met along the way. They taught me what true passion, motivation and advocacy look like, and I will be forever grateful to my STOY family.

The long hours a teacher puts in outside of the classroom are often in place of spending time with loved ones. I want to thank my daughter, Samara, and son, Salazander, for always being my cheerleaders and for giving me the inspiration to reach my goals. Thank you to my parents, Steve and Mary Juelke, for helping to pick up the slack and for instilling within me the values of hard work and compassion from a young age.

To all of the inspirational educators and community members, I have had the privilege of working with, especially my team of educators within the Fargo Public Schools, thank you for your dedication to education. The teachers, paras, administrators, counselors, social workers, SROs, maintenance staff, nutrition services and everyone in between make up an exceptional team that I am proud to be a part of.

The biggest sentiments of gratitude go out to my amazing students. Those that I taught in a boarding school in Taiwan, a private school in Ecuador, a charter school in Colorado and my current public school in North Dakota. I am who I am, because of them. I will forever carry the lessons that I have learned over the years from my diverse groups of students close to my heart. My students have taught me more about resilience, acceptance and love than I could have ever imagined. It is for them that I continue to do what I do. It is for them that I wrote these chapters, in hopes that other educators learn how to welcome our new EL students with open arms and open hearts.

–Leah Juelke

I will forever be grateful to my parents, Rosita and Jorge Mayorga, for making the sacrifice to immigrate to the U.S. to provide me with a brighter future and for being persistent about not losing my native language. I owe my ability to be bilingual to them. The gift of speaking Spanish has allowed me to make meaningful connections with so many students and families. ¡Mil gracias! I would also like to thank my husband, Mario Monterrey, and daughters Samari and Marisa for their support, patience and understanding in all of my endeavors. ¡Los amo! A special thank you to my mother-in-law and father-in-law, Rolando and Gloria Monterrey, for their continued support. A huge thank you to Mandy, Ivonne and Leah; it has been an honor to work with you on this project. I'm thankful for my village; my family, friends, colleagues and students who inspire me and bring me hope for a brighter future.

–**Sarahí Monterrey**

# Introduction

By Mandy Manning

With more than 1 billion people learning English worldwide, English language educators are uniquely positioned to facilitate creating welcoming school environments and to help students navigate their new communities. We do this both inside and outside of our classrooms.

It's easy as language teachers to get caught up in the mechanics of English. Building lessons and units on form and the structure of the English language is tempting. After all, there are so many prescribed rules related to grammar and language patterns. How much simpler is our job if we can just teach students style and form? However, when we look at function. Really dig into why and how we use language. How language is culture and geography and connection. That's when engagement happens and when we are able to focus on language as a means for connection.

Using language as a vehicle for connection is how we ensure the learning that happens in our classrooms has relevance to our students' everyday lives and sets each of them on a path toward being happy and engaged community members. With our focus on connection, we ensure that every student feels welcome and that they belong in our schools and across our communities.

I have been an educator for 21 years. During the first seven years of my career, I spent four of those years teaching English Learners in other nations. I started in Armenia, teaching English as a foreign language as a Peace Corps volunteer, and then went on to teach English in Sapporo, Japan. I have taught in Texas and in New York and the last 11 years of my teaching career I taught English to newly arrived immigrants and refugees in the Newcomer Center.

DOI: 10.4324/9781003177333-1

The Newcomer Center is a specialized English Language Development program specifically designed for new immigrant and refugee students who test at a level one on our English language proficiency exam and who have never attended school in the United States. The Center is housed in a comprehensive high school. Students stay in the program from a single semester to a year depending on level of support needed and the focus is on learning the basic building blocks of language, academic language students will need in mainstream classes and, most importantly, provides a safe place for students to learn to navigate and transition to living and studying in the U.S.

Before I go further, I want to acknowledge my lens. I am a white woman who has spent most of her career teaching English Learners in the United States. While I have taught overseas and in several states in the U.S. my lens is influenced by my life and career mainly in Washington state. Each of the other authors of this text write through the lens of their respective backgrounds and experiences. We sincerely hope you will find value in our ideas and practices.

My experiences as an educator have shown me that as the world grows larger, we actually become closer together as neighbors. As English educators, language is our vehicle through which we connect our students across this global neighborhood.

Let's look at some basic stats of the shifting demographics worldwide and in the United States. War, persecution and violence displaced 71 million people in 2018 (Westerman, 2019). This is two million more than the year before, and a 65% increase over the last decade. 140 million more people face the same fate due to climate change by 2050. Displacement is a global crisis and 52% of those displaced are children. As a result, children on the move have missed, at last count, 1.5 million weeks of school (UNESCO, 2018). This last year of living in a pandemic has surely impacted these numbers even more.

Nearly one-fifth of the world's migrants live in the United States (Radford, 2019). More than 40 million people living in the U.S. were not born here. Roughly one in ten of our students nationwide are English Learners (NCES, 2021). Moreover, homelessness in the U.S. has increased 70% over the last decade and of the nearly one and a half million young people facing housing instability, 16% are English Learners (Camera, 2019).

Over the last several years, our nation has taken a hard line on asylum-seekers, and this shift has devastated many immigrant children and their families. The U.S. is developing and enacting policies to reject refugees and asylum-seekers. Our government is preventing more people from finding safe-haven as they are forced to flee their homes. In 2016–17, we received the most refugees we ever had in a single year, 84,995, while in 2018–19 we welcomed 22,491 and in 2019–20 we welcomed even fewer, 11,800 (MPI, 2021). With a backlog of 1.1 million asylum-seekers awaiting adjudication in the U.S., President Biden proposes resettling only 15,000 refugees in 2021 (U.S. Department of State, 2020). We have incarcerated tens of thousands of children and separated countless children from their mothers and their fathers simply because they were not born in the United States (UNESCO, 2018). Over the last several years we've witnessed mass deportation, even deporting unaccompanied children.

Not only are our English Learners facing a massive transition to living and studying in this nation, they are also faced with the fear that they will be unwelcome and also turned away at a moment's notice.

These are the realities our English Learners face in our schools because they are immigrants. These facts also illustrate the need for English educators to focus on ensuring our schools are welcoming and that we view language as a vehicle for connection. When English Learners understand not only the mechanics of English, but also the culture of how language is used, they are able to navigate their community, and connect with their new neighbors, which leads to a sense of being welcome, and more success in their new lives.

Hussein came to the United States as a refugee from Iraq. When he entered my classroom in the fall of 2012, he had already turned 20. Often, at this age, students will choose to go to adult education, but Hussein decided, instead, to go to high school.

In his wisdom, he knew he would better be able to practice his English and learn about U.S. culture. Part of this was simply Hussein's personality. He is gregarious and outgoing, eager to learn English and be part of this new community, and he enjoys making new friends. The other part was that he yearned for connection.

That's always been our focus in the Newcomer Center, connection. We welcomed him into our classroom and helped him become part of our school community and our classroom family.

During his one year in the Newcomer Center, I knew we needed to do something a bit different for this unique young man. Hussein shared with us about his life before coming to the United States. Through those stories, I learned that he was a barber for the U.S. army in Baghdad, and that this was his ultimate dream to become a stylist.

While it was outside of the norm, I arranged with the skills center, our district's vocational program, for Hussein to attend cosmetology classes. He attended his classes there in the afternoon, then every morning he would come to school and we would sit together and review what he had learned the previous day with a particular focus on the language for cosmetology, not only the academic language but how he would communicate with his clients and his colleagues. By the close of that year, Hussein had gained hours toward his license and was set on a path toward success in his new community.

That year brought many challenges for Hussein, not only academically, but also personally, including being homeless for a time. Because of his connections with us in the Newcomer Center and the connections we helped him make outside of the classroom, he was able to navigate those difficulties, and come through on the other end with his potential and his belief in himself intact. In 2016, Hussein became a licensed cosmetologist and has a successful cosmetology business in Seattle, where he is also making music and working as a DJ.

If we had only focused on form and structure of English in Hussein's education, he may not be where he is today. Because we emphasized language as a vehicle for connection and culture, Hussein grew confident, became part of his new community and is now able to navigate that community, not assimilating to U.S. culture, but maintaining and celebrating who he is and the culture he brought with him, while at the same time becoming an integral part of the community, both giving of his talents and receiving the opportunities living in the U.S. affords him.

I am still in contact with Hussein today and we often discuss the state of immigration in the U.S. Hussein is now a citizen, but still fears for his place in his community because of the anti-immigrant policies and rhetoric in our nation. He is thankful he came in 2012 when we were welcoming refugees.

I recently had occasion to sit down and talk with Hussein. We talked about his experiences in the Newcomer Center and his journey that year. What I learned from that conversation was that it wasn't the leg up in pursuing his cosmetology license, or the one-to-one academic support we provided in the Newcomer Center that made the difference for him. It was the community we built, our commitment and follow-through, our encouragement to take risks and help in navigating the new culture in which he lived.

We believed in him, which helped him believe in himself. He stayed focused and committed even after aging out of high school, because he felt welcome, important and believed that he could make it in his new community.

With every new student who enters my classroom, I work to ensure they feel welcome. I figure out what each student needs in order to effectively transition to life and study in the U.S. That means actively listening and observing. Ensuring that I am open to all of my students' different ways of being, thinking and doing, accepting them, welcoming them and meeting them where they are. In getting to know our students as learners and as individual human beings, it is the follow-through and commitment that speaks to our students most and models for them the skills they need to make connections and to persevere.

This is all the more reason to focus on connection in our instruction and ensuring our students not only feel welcome and that they belong, but are able to effectively navigate their new home, confidently, as contributing members of our communities.

## Our Economic Landscape

U.S. immigration policy has a deep impact on our English Learners and building connection through language instruction helps them to find a sense of belonging in a nation which doesn't always feel welcoming. There are other challenges, as well. Our economic landscape is a big one.

In the U.S. the top 1% earns more than the bottom 50% (Beer, 2020). While our industries and our economic system depend on the work of our lowest paid people, low-wage workers who are often invisible and largely undervalued. This directly impacts our immigrant community.

Economic inequity leads to a negative impact on access. Those in lower socio-economic situations, such as residing in low-income neighborhoods and/or working in low-wage jobs often lack access to technology, whether actual tech, like individual devices, or access to high-speed internet and phone data plans.

There is also an impact on access to transportation. Many communities lack robust public transit systems and many people cannot afford their own vehicles or the associated costs of owning a vehicle. Tech and transportation access is also an issue in rural communities, creating a rural versus urban divide.

Our communities and our schools are rife with inequity and upward mobility is often non-existent for our most marginalized and oppressed communities, of which English Learners are one.

The Coronavirus pandemic has shined a neon light on these economic inequities. It is clear based on the U.S. response to shutting down for the health of our communities that our economic system depends on service workers, who are usually the lowest paid. Our economic system depends on our immigrant community and this directly impacts what and how we teach.

The families of my students are excellent examples of the value immigrant families bring to our communities, not only in terms of diverse ways of thinking, being and doing, but also their positive economic impact.

Safa came to the U.S. as a refugee from Sudan in 2012. She faced many challenges when she came into my classroom. As a result of her family's journey, she had severely interrupted education and had only completed the fourth grade. She was entering our school system as a freshman, in a newcomer class, which means she tested at a level one on our state's language proficiency assessment, and she carried the expectation that she would graduate from high school in four years. While this goal seems insurmountable, Safa did it. But Safa's story is not only about her. It is about the value her family brings to our community.

Safa is the only daughter of ten children. Her father labors on the production floor of a local farm equipment factory, a major industry and economic catalyst in my state. Most workers in the factory are immigrants, reflecting the fact that 17% of the U.S. civilian labor force is made up of immigrants (Collins, 2019). Immigrants have provided half the growth in our workforce in the past decade. As the number of refugees declines, positions like those in the farm equipment factory cannot be filled, impacting production and weakening our economy.

Safa's siblings are academically successful, and of the three oldest, one is currently attending university and the other two just graduated university. Safa's oldest brother is a McNair scholar and completed degrees in political science and international affairs. Safa, the second oldest in her family, graduated with her bachelor's degree in international affairs with a focus on global security. Most of the family members, including Safa, have now become naturalized citizens.

Every year I witness firsthand the optimism, the struggle, the determination, the trauma, the civic participation, the prejudice and the community involvement of the families who pass through my classroom. The issues are complex, but the lived experiences of my students and their families are real. Their ability to use education to better themselves and their new home is just as real. Immigrants make tremendous contributions to the economic success of this nation.

Safa benefited from the English language instruction she received in my class and in her others, but her language instruction alone is not the only factor in her success. When we use English language instruction as a vehicle for connection and focus on creating welcoming schools, we extend our lessons beyond the classroom. This means, we as English educators reach outside of our classrooms, and use English to connect our English Learners with mainstream students and members of the larger community. Not only does this benefit English Learners in receptive and productive elements of language, but it also exposes them to the new culture in which they live. Most importantly, this language exchange exposes community members and peers born in the United States to the beauty and culture our newest community members bring with them when they immigrate here. Language is an opportunity for cultural exchange.

## The Face of Hate

This brings me to another prevalent issue facing our schools and communities and an additional reason to recognize the value of focusing on connection and creating welcoming environments. Racial and social justice in the United States is the driver of our history and continues to have major impacts on our society.

Black Lives Matter demonstrations regularly occur across our nation and internationally. These demonstrations are born of the racial and social inequities in the U.S. that preserve white supremacist power structures and oppress communities of color, particularly Black communities. These inequities and systems of oppression are prevalent in every facet of U.S. society and schools.

These inequities have led to a new record of mass shootings every year. This has grown to be the new normal in our communities, even in our schools. There has been an increase in hate crimes, targeting Muslims and Jewish faith communities, those with heritage from Spanish-speaking countries, our trans community members, particularly trans people of color, anti-immigrant hate and most recently, an uptick in anti-Asian hate due to the coronavirus pandemic (Balsamo, 2020).

These systemic inequities have also led to significant youth incarceration (ACLU, 2021). In our schools, Black students are four times as likely to be suspended from school and 1.9 times for likely to be expelled than their white peers (Reuters, 2016). Additionally, incarceration of immigrant youth has increased exponentially and has led to an inordinate number of unaccompanied youth in our English language programs (Colorín Colorado, 2021).

Racial and social inequities have led to increased bullying and the consistent message that young people should live in fear, fear for their personal safety and fear for their futures. This can lead to a lack of agency and young people feeling powerless, fueled by lacking a sense of belonging.

The racial and social landscape are particularly difficult for our English Learners to navigate, especially when they are new to our nation. They don't know the depth of the impact of our racial history or our systems and are often trapped within systems of oppression that they didn't expect. This has been the case for many of my students. Here is one story that is particularly relevant today.

Jeff came to the U.S. as an asylum seeker through temporary protective status from Haiti. He came with substantial education, but his language proficiency was low, so he started in the Newcomer Center. Jeff is outgoing and motivated. He took extra classes in the summer and graduated a mere two and a half years after arriving in the United States.

Jeff became an Act Six scholar and received a full-ride scholarship to attend a local university. Along with the scholarship came four years of support through Act Six. During my year as National teacher of the year, I asked Jeff to speak at a few of my events. It was so fun reconnecting with him and learning about his post-high school experiences.

At university, Jeff studied sociology and hopes to one day become a school counselor. He explained that he wanted to be the type of counselor he needed as a Black English Language Learner and immigrant.

Jeff is spectacular, like most of my former students. He graduated in 2019 with his university degree. But, even Jeff, a self-starter with an incredible work ethic and an ever-optimistic outlook, almost didn't make it. He explained to me that before moving to the U.S., he had never been defined by the color of his skin. In Haiti, he was always just Jeff, measured by his actions, not by the way he looked. This new experience, the assumptions people made about him and the way they treated him because he has Black skin, was shocking and difficult for him to navigate.

Luckily, he said, he had his cohort and his support system both in high school through the English Language Development program, and at university through Act Six. Otherwise, he said, he wouldn't have made it. His skin color would have defined him because that's how he was viewed.

For me that was a heartbreaking story. And one that made it even clearer the importance of creating welcoming schools. It is why we must not only teach grammar and structure, but we must also teach culture and use English language instruction to help students navigate the world around them and make connections with the people who live beside them and across the globe.

There is hope in our practice as educators. There is so much for our students and for us as English educators to consider and navigate in our classrooms and in our planning for instruction. Beyond that, we must also work beyond our walls to impact our schools and our school districts in how we welcome English Learners. One thing is clear, English proficiency is our goal, but not in the sense of perfect form and structure, but rather English proficiency in connecting with our neighbors and our communities. The ability to use language to connect across cultures and also to navigate our diverse communities.

What follows in this book are our ideas and examples of how to intentionally welcome and celebrate English Learners in our educational environments. Each of us teaches in a unique context, comes from different backgrounds and we each have a multitude of different experiences. We hope our stories, practices and examples help you reflect and inspire you to create the most welcoming environment for the students in your community.

## References

ACLU. (2021). America's Addiction to Juvenile Incarceration: State by State. Retrieved from www.aclu.org/issues/juvenile-justice/youth-incarceration/americas-addiction-juvenile-incarceration-state-state.

Balsamo, M. (2020, November 16). Hate Crimes in U.S. Reach Highest Level in More Than a Decade. Retrieved from https://apnews.com/article/hate-crimes-rise-FBI-data-ebbcadca8458aba96575da905650120d.

Beer, T. (2020, October 8). Top 1% of U.S> Households Hold 15 Times More Wealth Than Bottom 50% Combined. Retrieved from www.forbes.com/sites/tommybeer/2020/10/08/top-1-of-us-households-hold-15-times-more-wealth-than-bottom-50-combined/.

Camera, L. (2019, February 21). Number of Homeless Students Soars. Retrieved from www.usnews.com/news/education-news/articles/2019-02-21/number-of-homeless-students-soars.

Collins, L. (2019, March 29). America Should Naturalize More Immigrants to Benefit Economy. Retrieved from https://thehill.com/opinion/immigration/435308-america-should-naturalize-more-immigrants-to-benefit-economy.

Colorado, C., (2021). Unaccompanied Children in Schools: What You Need to Know. Retrieved from www.colorincolorado.org/unaccompanied.

MPI. (2021, May 13). Refugees and Asylees in the United States. Retrieved from www.migrationpolicy.org/article/refugees-and-asylees-united-states-2021.

NCES. (2021, May). English Language Learners in Public Schools. Retrieved from https://nces.ed.gov/programs/coe/indicator/cgf.

Radford, J. (2019, June 17). Key Findings About U.S. Immigrants. Retrieved from www.pewresearch.org/fact-tank/2019/06/17/key-findings-about-u-s-immigrants.

Reuters. (2016, June 7). Black Students More Likely to be Suspended: U.S. Education Department. Retrieved from www.reuters.com/article/us-usa-education-suspensions/black-students-more-likely-to-be-suspended-u-s-education-department-idUSKCN0YT1ZO.

UNESCO (2018). *Migration, Displacement and Education: Building Bridges, Not Walls*. Paris: UNESCO.

U.S. Department of State. (2020). Report to Congress on Proposed Refugee Admissions for Fiscal Year 2021. Retrieved from www.state.gov/reports/report-to-congress-on-proposed-refugee-admissions-for-fy-2021/.

Westerman, A. (2019, June 19). Nearly 71 Million People Forcibly Displaced Worldwide as of 2018, U.N. Report Says. Retrieved from www.npr.org/2019/06/19/733945696/nearly-71-million-people-forcibly-displaced-worldwide-in-2018-says-u-n-report.

# Part 1

# From English Language Learner to Educator

*By Ivonne Orozco Sahi*

# 1

# Through the Lens of an English Language Learner

I did not become a teacher because it was a calling, rather, it was an accident. My family immigrated when I was 12 years old and I was in the seventh grade. A short six years after having arrived in the United States from Mexico, I graduated at the top of my high school class from a small, rural town in central New Mexico. Still, I lacked basic knowledge of the way education worked.

American schools were just like I had seen on television, the classrooms were inside and connected by shiny tiled hallways that were lined with lockers—yes, lockers and I got one all to myself and I could store my jacket in there—it was incredible. Middle school would be better than I ever imagined—at least so I thought, in the very narrow view of an almost teenaged girl.

One of the first conversations I remember in school in the U.S. was with a very nice woman, maybe she was a teacher, secretary, librarian, or educational assistant—I don't know. But she was one of two people who spoke Spanish at the middle school where I was about to be enrolled by my mother and my aunt, who had already lived in the States for many years and was helping us with the process. During the conversation with this woman, the adults in the room were trying to figure out my interests. "Do you like to sing?" she asked me in Spanish, I shook my head no. "Do you like to draw?" The adults in the room all looked at me, expectant this was the right choice—I actually did like to

DOI: 10.4324/9781003177333-3

draw a lot. I shook my head no anyway. I wasn't sure what she was getting at, but I wasn't about to start agreeing with her. The adults in the room laughed nervously, in a way that said, "Kids, what are you gonna do?"

My schedule ended up being composed of all the regular core classes for seventh grade: New Mexico History, English, Math, Science, etc. my electives ended up being Spanish class, which I loved, and PE and HomeEc, which I didn't love quite as much. Now reflecting back, I realize that the woman was trying to help me to pick some interesting electives—but with that process being entirely new to me (there are no electives in La Secundaria in Mexico, everyone simply takes the same subjects) I had ended up in classes that were not entirely my favorite.

I still look back at that conversation and wish I had nodded yes when I was asked about art class, about liking to draw. Years later, as I tried to figure out a major and minor at the University of New Mexico—a very similar but almost opposite thing would happen. My lack of knowledge of the American education system would lead me to take many classes I enjoyed but did not need. It is almost as if I overcorrected the misstep of not choosing the right electives back in middle school.

Even though I had been a 4.0 GPA student who kept a daily planner and never missed a single class or assignment, I had no idea that credit hours added up to a degree. By the time I was a junior in university without a concrete plan for graduation, I had to pick a path. One of my teachers and greatest mentors from high school, Mr. Kennedy, said to me "Why don't you become a teacher?" and my journey began.

The next three chapters are the story of me becoming the teacher and advocate for immigrant students that I am today. Along the way, I point out strategies and best practices not because I assume you need them, but because you may find some-thing that speaks to you in them. I do not have all the answers or knowledge. I simply have experience in the American education system as a student navigating learning English, being undocu-mented, being the first in my family to apply to college, becoming a teacher, then being selected as a State Teacher of the Year. This propelled my career as a teacher into becoming an advocate both inside and outside of my classroom. This work takes intentionality. It is beautiful, but sometimes also painful and raw. I have learned to show up whole to all the spaces I occupy and this book is one of them.

## The Power of Mentors and Teachers

My experience as an English Learner (EL) in rural America was filled with moments of personal perseverance while also being supported by teachers, coaches and counselors. After my initial seventh grade year, my family and I moved one town over, so I was enrolled in eighth grade in a new school. Once I became a teacher, I was actually hired at a charter school in Albuquerque being run by my former high school principal. In our conversations as educators, she let me know that there had been no English Language Learning program in the rural district before. They'd had to cobble together services to support students like me.

To my recollection, there were three other students in my English as a Second Language (ESL) class in the eighth grade, it was at the end of the day and we had a wonderful, kind teacher who spoke Spanish and helped us with our homework and assignments we had collected but not completed throughout the day.

This was the early 2000s and instant messaging chats were very popular, and even though while we were in class, we did not have the capabilities of IMing, the shortcuts of language would spill into middle school writing. One girl who would become one of my best friends, would pass me notes written in a sparkly purple pen during our history class. They were long and included much of the social drama that goes on in a small middle school. I quickly learned the meaning of "crush," "boyfriend" and "clique," but there was one word that kept coming up in the clandestine notes being passed under desks while we learned about the Constitution that I didn't understand. The word was "LOL" in all caps. I did not know this word. I looked it up in my pocket English-Spanish dictionary but it was not there. I had no choice, I had to ask my ESL teacher to help me with this very important quest for meaning. To my disappointment, my teacher was not sure what LOL meant either. I wrote it on the whiteboard, "Así, todo en mayúsculas," "like this, in all caps," I said to her. "No sé…," she said, thinking about it. Then she said, "Maybe, lots of love?" That was of no help, it did not fit the context, but I moved on.

I do not remember the exact moment when I learned the real meaning of laughing out loud, but I do remember hanging on to the feeling that my ESL teacher had no idea what she was talking about in regards to language, which she was supposed to be teaching me, or about culture. This is one of the first times in my young life that I remember realizing that teachers may not know everything, like I expected. In the way that we often generalize when we are barely teenagers, I assumed that she probably would not know much of anything else I asked or wondered. My reluctance to ask questions grew, I felt the teacher had been so out of touch and the trust I had in her to guide me through the world of English Language Learning diminished. As a teacher now, I try to keep up with language trends and figure out what exactly it means when someone points to the inside of their arm, or the "ice in my veins" trend on TikTok, to say that they're feeling cool under pressure. Because even though it seems like something crazy only the young kids are doing, there may be a student who asks, "Ms. Orozco, what does that mean?" and I want to be ready with the answer, or at least the humility to say, you know what, I don't know but let's find out together.

Teachers have incredible power, as the adults at the front of the room. Students, particularly EL students, are learning from us, imitating us, repeating our cadence, vocabulary, tone, gestures and yes—our views of the world. This is why it is so important to watch what we say, do and the ways we communicate our beliefs, especially when we think about our students and their abilities. Therefore, we should strive to listen attentively, ask questions and become a reflection of what we learn from our students. Showing that their views and knowledge have value to us.

As an EL student, I have so many formative moments in which teachers played a role in the ways in which I think about the world. A few weeks ago, my two-year-old daughter asked me to "make her leche" by which she means me putting a cup of whole milk in the microwave for a minute to warm it up and pouring it in the sippy cup her dentist said she should not use any more. I looked at her and said, "Poof! You are leche now!" My wife who was also in the kitchen laughed at my corny joke and I followed with a triumphant explanation of this being a Mrs. Walker joke.

Mrs. Walker was my ninth grade Pre-AP English teacher and she truly believed in my writing. She was fun and energetic, and best of all—she never expected less of me because English was my second language. I once asked her to "make me a note" for whatever reason, probably to go to the office or the Yearbook room where I loved to hang out, and she followed with the "Poof! You are a note!" joke.

My wife chuckled at my story and then said, "Right, but that joke is from *Singing in the Rain.*" I was baffled, all of this time I thought Mrs. Walker was an original joke teller. I had waited over a decade to deliver the joke in the way she did when I was in her classroom. Now, I come to find out that Mrs. Walker's wit was borrowed from one of America's film classics. But in my mind, for all these years, Mrs. Walker's way of teaching, loving and using corny puns had been inspiring. Students are always watching and repeating what they learn from us, even if it is years, and years down the road.

As I mentioned, my ninth-grade English teacher stood out to me because she was a wonderful teacher and as such, she never treated me as less than the rest of her students, even though I had only been speaking English for two years. Teachers like her contributed so much to my sense of belonging in school. There were several anchors that kept me grounded as I made my way through high school as an EL but also highly social, and academically successful student.

In my ninth-grade year I joined the track team and after that, I started running long distances in the summer to prepare for the cross country season in the fall. I was approached by other runners in my track team and since we were such a small school, they were desperate to find five girls willing to join the team so we could qualify to run in meets. I was never fast or very good at running but I loved being on that team. I loved being part of cross country, I made wonderful friendships with my teammates and best of all, I was mentored by my coach Laci Lockwood. Coach Lockwood had a way of bringing athletes together, having us run as individuals but also taking pride in being a team. I had never felt more seen and encouraged than I did running as part of her team.

Academically, I was mentored through challenging chemistry and physics classes by my teacher Roger Kennedy. Mr. Kennedy is my mentor even to this day, and yes, he was the one who encouraged me to teach. In his classes, we learned about chemistry, the solar system, mathematics and pop culture references like the band ABBA, which I had never heard about before. Mr. Kennedy was overjoyed to share and build knowledge with his classes.

He was one of the first adults I confided in about my immigration status. I was undocumented so I knew my path to higher education would be different than that of my classmates. Mr. Kennedy soon became an expert in all New Mexico legislature that would allow me to go to college and the way I could still apply for private, non-federal scholarship money. He talked to the counselor at my high school and brought him in on the part about my life I did not let any of my friends know about. Together, they worked on ways to encourage me to take the ACT, apply to scholarships and to the University of New Mexico. I am so grateful for their help, resources, and knowledge of the systems that I needed to navigate to get to the next level in my education.

Perhaps the biggest takeaway from these teachers is that they all believed in me, they recognized something that they saw worth and value in. If they didn't know the answer, they would find the resources for me. They always made me feel like I was one of their own. I never felt othered in these spaces, I was always welcomed and they were willing to fight for me. When I think about my own students now, I hope that they see in me that I am here to fight for them, to find answers and resources and to always believe in their worth.

Being that type of teacher requires us to think of students as whole people with a story, a story we must give space for our students to tell us about. The way I create space in my classroom for that to happen includes little things like pronouncing names correctly, and when they say "Oh, it doesn't matter" I say, "But how does your family pronounce it?" then they tell me, and I practice saying it right so that the next time they see me they notice the effort.

Another quick way to appreciate students' background is to notice their pronunciation of Spanish words, when their accent is particularly well executed I say things like, "Did you grow up hearing Spanish? Who in your family speaks it?" There are usually one or two people in their family who do, sometimes an entire side of their family speak it and students want to desperately be part of that world and language is their way in. We practice practical phrases they can use with family-like complimenting food or reactions in social contexts. When their Spanish accent is particularly harsh, really struggling, I'll say something like, "We gotta keep working on that, tell me about your family, does anyone speak Spanish?" their answer is typically no, which I already knew, and I'll say, "What motivates you to be here?" Sometimes, it is just a credit for graduation, other times it is travel or their friend's family who speaks Spanish and we dig a little bit there. Either way, I have learned something about them, then I bring that back a couple of days later, "Well you know, Marisol's entire mom's side of her family speaks Spanish, so she wants to connect with them" or "Kevin's family doesn't speak Spanish at all, so he's the ambassador there, he's the one teaching his whole family colors this week, right Kevin?" Those connections, seeing students for who they are, is what makes a classroom into a community. And once there is a community, there is confidence in our ability to support students in academics and beyond. Once students know that we care about who they are, they confide in us with bigger things like immigration status and we can be of support there too.

Teachers often take on so many things not on their job description so that they can support students, however the system may sometimes create barriers for teachers to act on their caring.

I was supported academically by individuals but also got caught up in the system that is often unfair to EL students and other marginalized students. For example, in my eighth-grade year I tested into the pre-algebra class but this was mostly due to my language skills instead of my mathematical skills, which means that in high school I took the Algebra 1, Geometry, Algebra II, Trigonometry track. If I had been tested purely on my math skills, and not language, I may have tested into Algebra 1 in my eighth-grade year, which in turn, would have led to the Geometry, Algebra II, Trigonometry, Calculus track. This systemic decision to place me in a different math class led to me not having the sufficient mathematical skills to then take higher-level mathematics while I was in university. Although I took high levels of science classes like Advanced Chemistry and Advanced Physics in high school, and I had strong math skills to go along with the subject matter, I had already been placed in the "track."

We often do this to students, whether they are EL, special education, or other marginalized groups. Schools do students a disservice by pigeonholing them to classes due to a tracking system that is antiquated. Instead, we should place students in academically challenging classes each year and not simply "the next one" in the curricula that have been set by the district. I see this pan out often in Spanish classes; students who are already bilingual speakers and readers will be placed in my Spanish 1 class, Spanish as a world language, which disserves these students who need a more challenging curriculum like that of Spanish III or AP Spanish. However, there is fear to move students into those classes in what is considered a premature timing, so they're placed in the same track as English monolingual students—they end up being bored and losing interest in a class that should affirm their culture and who they are. As a department at my current school, we try to catch these schedule mistakes early and work closely with our counselors to request schedule changes, although often requests are denied since other classes are full or it doesn't fit the master schedule. I find the process frustrating and exhausting, yet it is one that we must engage in every single year, to make sure our students are receiving the education they deserve.

## Losing Myself to Assimilation

Even though I found myself surrounded by supportive, English-speaking, white adults, one part that was substantially lacking was my sense of self. I wanted badly to fit in, to assimilate and be just another teenager growing up in a small town in America. I worked at concealing my Spanish accent even though I had only spoken English for a few years. I got involved in many extracurriculars and made friends with white kids whose families were Republican, Christian and xenophobic. Although I seemingly fit in since I constantly pushed my true self away. Still, in the best days I was my friends' "Mexican best friend," my nationality and race were always a qualifier in the title. For years I tried to fit into a mold not designed for me.

The busier I was in school, the less I shared with my family at home. I truly thought they would just not understand what I was going through, a commonly held belief by a teenager. But there was something deeper, I actually did not have the Spanish vocabulary to explain to my family all that I was doing. I lacked words like: cross country meet, State Tournament, National Honor Society, volunteering, yearbook, Business Professionals of America, business applications, youth group (which I attended with my formerly mentioned Christian Baptist friends even though my family was Catholic).

In the chaos that was my daily schedule as an overachieving teenager, I stopped sharing with my family at home the reasons I was so busy. I stopped communicating the things that were important to me, and I divided myself more and more each time I avoided telling my family about momentous events like winning an essay competition or being selected as editor of the yearbook. I became the cliché story of being too Mexican to be American but too American to be fully Mexican.

It is crucial that we give our EL, immigrant and refugee students the resources to keep on communicating with their families about their academic and extracurricular lives. Part of this is providing some academic vocabulary in the language our students speak. It would have made a huge difference for me to have known how to say things as simple as "essay" or "research project" but because I did not have these words, I ended up sharing with my parents—if at all—in a mix of Spanglish: "Hola mamá, tengo un *cross country meet* de *district* el sábado. Estoy nerviosa porque podemos hacer *qualify* para *State*." Because my mother did not understand cross country meet, district, qualify or state, she was left in the dark about why districts were so important in a cross country season, something that had been central to my training for the previous several months. It is not at all that my parents did not care about my student-athlete life. In fact, my mom made burritos for my entire Cross Country team on numerous occasions all three years that I ran. But, because I didn't have the tools to talk to my parents about what was so important to me, they ended up only knowing the part they understood—I would be somewhere Saturday and they would drop me off and pick me up.

As educators, we need to ensure that our students do not deep dive into assimilation, the way I did, and leave behind their families and communities thinking they somehow do not fit together. If I could go back in time, I would ask my coach or a teammate to help me make a list of words that we knew because we ran cross country and I would translate those to Spanish and have them readily available when speaking to my parents about what I was doing. It is what I do now, actually. I often have to look up education words so I can tell my mom what is going on in my professional life—which happens in English. I have gotten better at advocating for my own vocabulary to strengthen my voice and relationships with my Spanish-speaking community, but I wish I had some help doing that back when I was 15 years old.

## Welcoming Environments Depend on Both Individuals and Systems

The New Mexico State Bill 582, which passed in 2005, states that "A public post-secondary education institution shall not deny admission to a student on account of the student's immigration status." New Mexico is a wonderful place that truly has opened many doors for me, and bills such as this one assured me that I could continue my education beyond high school. I owe so much to the incredible community advocates who did this work for decades so that I could have an opportunity at higher education, something that is not available to all undocumented youth depending on which state they live in. However, NMSB582 shows that when we work to advocate for inclusive legislation, that work makes an impact on real people and communities.

The U.S. Citizenship Act signed by President Joe Biden has many needed changes that advocates have been working toward for a very long time now. One of those changes, and it might seem insignificant and not nearly as impactful as the rest of the bill that outlines a path to residency and citizenship for undocumented people in the United States, is to replace the word "alien" with "noncitizen" in our immigration laws, as the bill further recognizes America as a nation of immigrants. I currently have an "alien number" and this small but rather symbolic change is so meaningful to me. The New Mexico State Bill 582 and the U.S. Citizenship Act are proof that this country believes in the journey of immigrants like me and like the countless immigrant students in our classrooms, especially those who are noncitizens.

Of course, state and national legislation are important, but this extends beyond government and into our institutions. Systems have to be addressed, as well. With the help of teachers and mentors, I applied and was accepted to the University of New Mexico. Which was about an hour and a half drive from the small town where I lived. It was culturally challenging for me to leave home to study. My parents had a hard time with the decision, as many young Mexican women, especially from my parents' generation, are expected to live at home until they are married, but at the end of the day we decided a commute would be too arduous and I would be safe living on campus.

As any 17-year-old, I was excited to live in the dorms and have some independence away from home. During my campus tour right before I moved in, I found myself being as excited about it as I had been about my seventh-grade locker, and it was just like the movies once again, with a cafeteria that served food until late hours of the night, meal plans, a recreation room, clubs and sports to play right outside my door. I had gotten many private, small scholarships that would cover my tuition for my first year, and with the help of my parents, we were able to pay for my room and board as well.

One day, I was on a phone call to get things settled with the Housing office at the university, when the woman I was talking to asked for my social security number over the phone so she could look up my account. I panicked, "I don't have one," I said to her as calmly as I could, but in the back of my mind I was thinking, could she deny my admission if she finds out I am undocumented? Worse, would I be deported if she told immigration? Is my family in danger now? To my surprise, she slightly chuckled and said, "Oh honey, everyone has a social security number, ask your mom for it." I said okay and quickly hung up.

I was horrified but glad she only thought I was a ditsy teenager instead of someone who was here without documents. Shortly after this incident, I was assigned a number by the university in lieu of a social security number and shortly after that, they stopped using social security numbers altogether and moved to solely using student ID numbers. I still have my ID number memorized from my college days. That number gave me normalcy. I was just like everyone else when I used it and I was so grateful.

Creating welcoming environments depends on both individuals and systems. Systems like using student ID numbers instead of social security numbers, and individuals like people who work in education: teachers, professors, clerical staff, to be aware that certain situations can be tricky for students and to approach these with a more delicate touch that allows students to keep their humanity. A more recent example of this was with a teacher colleague of mine who was frustrated with her Senior Advisory class, a few of her students still had not turned in the FAFSA even though she had walked them through it and given them several reminders. I mentioned to her that some students are not able to fill out the form for federal student aid because they may not qualify if they are undocumented, it is also worth mentioning that these types of applications are really difficult for students in the foster care system. She did not know that was something that could be a barrier for students. Sometimes, even just knowing information can be the best way to advocate for all of our students.

## Finding Community and Reclaiming My Self Identity

Once I was enrolled at the University of New Mexico, I was not aware that I needed to find myself and people like me—but it still happened. In my Spanish classes, I met other students whose Spanish was strong but did not know how to talk to their parents about the final exams schedule. I found out about El Centro de la Raza, the center on campus designed to support Latinx students and their specific needs. I hung out there more and more until I got a research internship called El Puente, which helped me understand the intricacies of future post-baccalaureate opportunities like graduate school.

I also joined Out Womyn, a group associated with the LGBT+ resource center on campus and I found community there. I took classes in the Chicano Studies department and I learned about the rich cultural history of New Mexico and the Civil Rights Movement that Cesar Chavez and Dolores Huerta had led. I read authors like Sandra Cisneros and Adrienne Rich and I just knew I had found my belonging. What is astonishing to me is that it took so many years of education to finally get to classes that were interesting and where the authors had experiences like mine. Texts in which I could see myself, whether through the experiences of a Mexican-American girl in The House on Mango Street or in the queer love poems that finally used the words I had been feeling for years.

Many times, when educators think about social-emotional learning or culturally responsive teaching, we think it will need a complete overhaul of what we already do. We think we have to reinvent the wheel completely. In reality, we can provide a more equitable curriculum by simply including diverse voices in our classes.

As I read more diverse authors and thought about myself within these contexts, my identity became stronger, and I learned, and learned and learned. I took full loads every semester, as much as my scholarships would pay for—18 credit hours. I took classes at the Honors College where I learned about historical artifacts, writing poetry, bird watching and programming apps. Through this wonderful journey of attending a state university, I had once again, mentors and professors leading me to become my full self.

At El Centro de la Raza, Dr. Virginia Necochea introduced me to Critical Race Theory and the way institutions have marginalized communities of color throughout history. At the Honors College, Dr. Ursula Shepherd pushed me to think about my future, particularly around immigration, and what my options were. She wrote me numerous letters of recommendation to private scholarships, and although I never read them, they were always in sealed envelopes covered by her script signature, and every time she wrote on my behalf, I received the aid I needed. I still check in with her every once in a while, and each time I do, I learn something from her. At the Spanish department, I was finally challenged to think about my first language and expand my vocabulary. The readings were sometimes so difficult that my mom had to read them out loud to me so that I could understand them.

It was a beautiful journey of self-actualization. Except for the part where I had no idea what I was doing. Yes, I was becoming the best version of myself, I was learning, growing, having fun, but I also did not understand the fundamentals of the institution. Credits need to add up to a degree. Because I had spent so much time taking a wide variety of classes, like Jogging Fitness and Nature Writing, I actually did not have any substantial number of credits in any one area. Well, kind of, I had enough credits at the Honors College to qualify for the newly approved Honors Interdisciplinary Studies Minor, and I also had many upper-level Spanish credits.

That is when my high school science teacher, Mr. Kennedy posed the question, "Why don't you become a teacher?" It made sense, I loved school, I loved the way my teachers and professors had led me to grow in so many aspects of my life, and it would also guarantee a career, which would be meaningful for my family. Once I made the decision and applied to the College of Education and Human Sciences at UNM, I found out that I would need two additional years of study, two semesters of course work and two semesters of student teaching, I decided to go for it.

Right around the time of this life-changing decision, there was another life-changing announcement made by President Barack Obama. The executive order that granted Deferred Action for Childhood Arrivals (DACA), which allowed young people like me who had arrived at this country as children, within limited criteria, to apply for deferred action from deportation and receive a work permit and social security number to be renewed every two years. Although I was skeptical of the announcement at first, once some of my friends started receiving their permits, I applied for mine as well.

The process was confusing, with a lot of legal language on forms that were lengthy and intimidating. It also costs nearly $500 to apply, which I did not have because I was a full-time student living off my meal plan and scholarships. My parents made it happen, I had the application checked by a free lawyer at the Mexican Consulate. I went through the background check with USCIS, and Mr. Kennedy came with me to my biometrics appointment where they took all of my fingerprints and picture. We both wore suits although it was clearly a much more casual occasion.

Finally, it came in the mail. I had a document that protected me from deportation and allowed me to work in the country I had called home for almost a decade. My parents and I cried. DACA was life-changing. I started working and getting paid as a tutor on campus, helping peers with their Spanish and writing homework. I had a concrete plan for after graduation. I would be able to work as a teacher in any public school. My immigration status would not be a barrier.

## Concluding Thoughts

I share my journey because it is so important that we're all doing the self-identity work that leads to seeing the humanity in ourselves. When you know who you are, then you can show up whole, with all of the pieces that make you yourself. You walk in as all of you to your classroom and your students sense it. You do it for them and for you. It is in this way that you can understand they're on their own journey of self-identity. The experiences they have lived so far and the formative moments they are having in your classroom have a lasting impact.

What will your students' stories of your classroom be 10, 15, 20 years from now? When you keep questions like this in mind, your purpose and intentionality become more clear. Will their memories be of love and inclusion, or fear and rejection? However, this work starts from within, keep on doing the work to see all the parts that make you who you already are, then move forward from there.

 ## Reflection Questions

Consider these questions as you think about your practice and pedagogy as you consider creating an inclusive school community for your immigrant and refugee students.

1. What are the stories that you remember about your teachers? When were they particularly inspiring or disappointing to you? What were the reasons for that?
2. What is the main memory of your teaching that you want students to have years after they leave your classroom?
3. What parts of yourself do you actively bring into the classroom? Which ones do you leave out?
4. What are some knowledge gaps that you may need to fill to better serve your immigrant and refugee students?
5. Where can you find this information? Or, if you have a lot of knowledge in this topic, how can you share that with colleagues and students?

# 2

# Being the Educator Immigrant Students Need

Teaching as a profession in the United States has historically been a space occupied by majority white women (Flores, 2011). For educators of color, the resistance, or the fight against the system that does not always reflect who we are, begins even just by walking into our own classrooms, we are the diversity our students deserve to see. When students see themselves reflected in the curriculum, and in their teachers, they can start connecting to the school community in deeper ways. However, education spaces can continue to be alienating for educators of color, so it is imperative that we create professional communities in which teachers and students of color are supported. There are countless books and resources that already tackle the role of white educators in this. You may want to read *So You Want to Talk about Race* and *How to be an Antiracist*.

As a first-year teacher, I felt the pressure all young teachers feel: to be competent, well-spoken, professional, knowledgeable, all while teaching, planning, attending meetings and being thrown into the deep end of a profession that you can only learn by doing. I became a Spanish teacher for high school students, and I was hired at a charter school in Albuquerque. I was the sole Spanish teacher, and only one of four Spanish speakers on campus. The other three people were clerical and custodial staff. I did not have a community of teachers to talk about curriculum

DOI: 10.4324/9781003177333-4

development. It was up to me and the loosely drafted national foreign language standards, which leave most content up to interpretation and focus on bigger picture skills such as communication, community, connections, cultures and comparisons. So, I relied heavily on my experience as an English Language Learner to in turn provide my students the skills, they needed to learn Spanish as their second language.

The range of language skills in my class varied greatly. Many of my students had never studied Spanish before, and my class was their first introduction to the ABC's and numbers 1–10 in Spanish. Other students had attended bilingual elementary programs and their skills were much more advanced. I also had students who only spoke Spanish at home, like me. I had students at these varying levels all in the same small portable classroom, with what would be considered a small section number of students. My pedagogy slowly evolved to be based on values and goals that can be fulfilled through the content and skills.

I want my classroom to be a space where students feel good about learning a second language, a place where they experience learning the language and feel like they can keep on learning after they leave my class. A place in which students can learn about cultures, Spanish-speaking and their own. A place that allows for the world to become full of possibility, where we can have difficult conversations about the world in which we live.

In September of 2017, Puerto Rico was hit by two major hurricanes, Irma and Maria. I knew a couple of the students in my Spanish classes had family in Puerto Rico, because we had engaged in dialogue about its rich history and culture. Some of my students shared that they still hadn't heard back from family members and were worried. This made the crisis that was going on in the Caribbean seem a lot more real to my classes than it would have been had we not had a real connection to people and place. Giving space for those conversations to happen is important and relevant to the way we think about the culture and people of Spanish-speaking communities.

As a Spanish teacher to mostly monolingual English speakers, I find that showing the beauty of Spanish-speaking countries is essential. Textbook companies are good at doing this, highlighting rainforests and festivals at the end of each chapter. But how can we take our lessons beyond that? How can we teach our students to recognize the bias in the stories we tell ourselves, as people living in the United States, about "others?" How can we get students to think about communities beyond natural habitats and festivals that we can attend as tourists? How can we teach them about what is important for the people from the countries of the language we are studying? This is a harder challenge. I am not criticizing using the textbooks (although outdated) that we are provided or talking about festivals that are important to the culture we're studying, rather, I am asking how we can go beyond those elements. How can we rethink curriculum and the colonialism mindset that we bring as educators in the Western world?

For me, one of these big moments was looking at our Spanish II curriculum map, which ended with a large unit on ancient cultures of Mesoamerica. It is an interesting topic that completely glossed over the fact that ancient cultures of Mesoamerica had their own flourishing languages, many of which survived the colonization by Spaniards who brought over disease, oppressing religion and murder. Many of these languages are being revitalized by the Native People of the regions, while other languages did not survive this traumatic and horrible "conquista" on the part of Spanish people.

How can we, as Spanish teachers, teach this topic without this historical background? How can we stay in the target language and grammar that we need to cover in a unit of ten lessons or less without doing a great disservice of not addressing these historical atrocities? I was not comfortable with teaching my students the sentence "Los Aztecas comían maíz y jugaban fútbol" or "*The Aztecs ate corn and played soccer*" simply for the use of imperfect past tense in description. So, I engaged my collaboration team in a discussion about our curriculum. Either we could reshape what this unit was about and make it about the reasons Spanish is such a prominent language around the world, or we could teach the imperfect past tense for description in a different unit.

We went with the latter option, it was easier, and made sense for us to stay on topic and in the learning targets we had set out for our Spanish II students. But the conversation had to happen, we needed to question why we were teaching the topic this way. I expected push back from my colleagues, I was ready with facts and counterarguments. To my surprise, they agreed with the points I made, and we changed our curriculum in a substantial way. As educators, it is our responsibility to not only teach the form and function of language but also the history of the language we are presenting. It is essential for our students to understand the way humanity is connected through time. Students benefit from a mindful curriculum by not being exposed to further stereotypes like the ones our curriculum previously presented about native cultures. As teachers, we benefit from the change in the curriculum by ensuring we stay true to our values.

*Reflection*: Think about your own curriculum—is there something that you know is problematic but keep doing because it is the way it is? Do you only read Black authors for Black History Month, but you know you could incorporate them throughout your curriculum because Black authors are just as valuable as the white authors you read the rest of the year? Do you only teach about white scientists and the way they discovered a certain theory, when in fact other cultures had a similar or the same concept for centuries before? What perspectives are we bringing in our classrooms and how are we making sure we show our values in each lesson we teach?

## Master of Arts in Education: Focus on Reflective Practice

As I have mentioned, I became a teacher by institutional mistake and luck. I think of teaching for me as a calling, something I was meant to do, but this doesn't mean that my commitment was immediate from the beginning. My second year teaching I was really struggling with my identity as a young teacher. I felt stuck, uninspired and I cried in my car after school on most days. One day, I called one of my undergraduate professors from U.N.M. and told her about my woes. She told me about an amazing M.A. program designed for current teachers. This program was appealing to me because it focused on giving current teachers an opportunity to reflect and grow on their current practice and use their own classrooms as the vehicles for learning. It was not a way out of my career as a teacher, but a way back to the profession where I knew my heart could thrive. And it was in this way that I recommitted myself to being a teacher, to learning about my craft and going deeper by asking questions of my practice and then answering them with my own field research.

I didn't have that skill before, the reflection piece of it—the lighting up as you think back on what a student said or what you yourself said. I was going through the motions, giving homework because I thought that is what schools should do. Working late because that is the narrative we are told as young teachers. I was exhausted and students pick up on this energy of despair. How do we get our students to come back and be us if we're not taking care of ourselves and cultivating the love for our profession? When we think about recruiting more teachers, this starts when future teachers are still in high school. Maybe if students saw their own teachers be respected by their community and saw teachers enjoy and love their job and lives outside school, they would want to come back and teach in their own classrooms. Going back for my M.A. brought that energy back for me, the inspiration that I hope I still share with my students when they walk into my class.

My Master's program asked us to observe, listen and uplift the voices and experiences of students in our classrooms. My inquiry project came to life in the spring of 2017 when I started focusing my attention on heritage language learners and their role in my traditional world language class curriculum. These are students that come into my Spanish class with oral skills and cultural knowledge but often can use some further development in academic vocabulary and reading and writing skills.

I started thinking about the ways in which my curriculum underserved these students, and how I wished that I could provide better differentiation and an opportunity to really build the skills they need. I was also doing a disservice to myself by not allowing my classroom to be a place where I was also allowed to grow and reflect on my own identity and experiences (hooks, 1994). I had put myself in a box where I taught phonics, grammar and language rules and I was leaving out so much culture, identity and love.

With this observation in mind, I proposed to the administration at my school a new class which would build a curriculum specifically for students who were heritage language learners of Spanish. My school principal was on board with the idea, although I was told that perhaps we wouldn't have the numbers to make a brand-new class. I set out to talk to students personally about why they should select this new class the following school year. At the time, I worked at a small charter school and ended up with 11 students registered—enough for the class to make. I had made a population that was previously invisible—visible.

When the class started in the Fall, we jumped right into class and I introduced a few short stories with vocabulary activities and seminar discussion questions. I was ready to finally give my students all they had not been able to have in previous years. I imagined a Spanish learning Utopia where students discovered the true meaning of their identities by comparing themselves to characters of color and seamlessly weaving metaphors and similes like never before.

And then…there was nothing. Well, not nothing, rather there was silence, hesitation. Some students answered the questions half-heartedly, others were simply not making eye contact, which was awkward because we were a very small group sitting in a circle. I couldn't figure out what was happening. We finally had a class designed for heritage language learners. I had the culturally relevant stories in my hand, and yet there was this silence in the room.

Listening to the silence, I realized that these students needed more than space, more than a class designed for them, they needed to get to know each other and feel *comfortable* in school. Oftentimes, students of color have experienced years and years of schools systematically crushing their spirit, telling them that they are not good enough or smart enough, or ever enough (Love, 2020), so I needed to figure out how to build comfort for populations of students of color. My master's inquiry project focused on how I could further understand the role of language learning in each student's identity development, name it and in so doing, counteract common language learning myths in my classroom. This would dispel language production anxiety and reduce language anxiety by creating community in our classroom.

I work to ensure that my classroom provides the space where language ties speakers to knowledge, culture and their identities. According to Mikulski (2006), heritage language learners who actively work on improving their language skills, report better relationships with families and see their skills as an asset to society. Language is a primordial part of what defines us as people. The development of language, especially a home language, can have lasting effects through our lives and for these reasons, students must be actively engaged in the content Heritage Language classes provide (Valdés, 1978). Nakkula and Toshalis (2016) argue that it is imperative for educators to move beyond understanding adolescent identity development and toward promoting such development in everyday interactions, as youth do not enter identity statuses alone, nor do they negotiate them independently, instead there are many factors and agents in the shaping of these identities. When I think about my own journey as a student developing all aspects of my identity, I am so grateful that I had teachers around me who believed in me and were quick to affirm all things that made me who I am.

Carreria (2007) argues that classes designed specifically for heritage learners may play a key role in narrowing the Latino achievement gap as these classes may serve as the bridge for students to support their Spanish-English biliteracy, facilitate learning across the curriculum, socialize students and their families to the American system of education and promote students' knowledge as resources in the classroom. These benefits are not to be taken lightly. In my classroom, students have engaged in conversations of what language learning means to them and some of the factors that may inhibit learning, such as language anxiety. We also discuss how language learning enhances their performance in class. We build a community of learners in our classroom. For me, as a teacher, it is so much more enjoyable to engage in teaching and learning with a group of students who are making connections from curriculum to personal experience and in turn sharing that with the class. For example, one year in one of my Spanish classes as we discussed the traditional celebration of a young person's fifteenth birthday or *quinceañera,* one of my students shared the fact that she had two quinceañeras, one here and one in Mexico. Several of her family members are not able to travel either from Mexico to the U.S. or vice versa, so her family had two parties so that the whole family could take part in the celebration. I could have explained to my students that sometimes families choose to have two celebrations, but it was so much more powerful coming from my student, then her sharing pictures and telling us about the baile sorpresa or surprise dance that she prepared with her cousins.

This is not to say that teaching heritage language learners does not come with its own set of challenges. A prominent language learning myth in the United States is the ideal of a *proper* version of Spanish—a more formal, more refined, more academic version that will transcend borders and be useful regardless of context. This myth is present in my classroom, and other classrooms I have observed, as it is propagated by families, teachers and world organizations alike. According to their website, in 1713, La Real Academia Española was founded with the principal mission of making sure that the changes the Spanish language undergoes do not break the essential unity the language provides amongst the Spanish-speaking world. La Academia is vigilant about the words that are included in the dictionary, which is perceived as *the standard* for the Spanish language. La Academia sends the message that Spanish must be approached in a standard way, and that anything beyond that may be considered improper and may harm the unity the language gives the world. While those wishing for a society of equality, rid of social prejudice may argue all languages and dialects are equally important, this may prove to be a difficult subject to breach. Teachers and students walk a fine line as they discuss the value of dialects and introduce the *standard* or more academic variety of the language due to the power associated with standard varieties. Leeman (2005) discusses the importance of recognizing the social status of languages:

> ...the claim that all language varieties have their appropriate place gives the false impression of equality among

varieties, thus obscuring the relationship between socio-economic power and the privileging of certain varieties and styles in high-status public domains. While it is certainly accurate that all language varieties are equally legitimate in linguistic terms, it is not the case that they have equal social status, nor that speakers of different varieties are treated equally.

(p. 38)

These dominant sociolinguistic hierarchies may deny students agency as they attempt to grapple not only with their own learning of the language, but also the structural ideologies at play in society regarding learning Spanish.

In my own classroom this matters because students must learn to recognize the structures of power that are at work with certain varieties of the language, while at the same time honoring the Spanish that is part of their daily lives. I work to ensure that through my class students will learn the power of code-switching amongst varieties of Spanish and the value all versions of the language have in their lives to start dispelling the myth of the lack of value of home language in classrooms.

One of the most powerful ways I have found in my classroom to correct these misperceptions of a *proper* version of Spanish or no value in language study is to assure students they are part of something bigger than themselves. Vygotsky (1980) argues that the two main forces driving cognitive development are social interaction and language, therefore the yearning to belong to a learning community is a natural inclination. In the language classroom, social interaction must be designed in an intentional way to build a community that supports learners and allows them to diminish their anxiety. Schaps (2003) stresses the value of building caring, inclusive and participatory communities within schools. He argues that the lasting benefits of strong school communities include higher academic motivation, the development of social and emotional competencies and helps to avoid many problem behaviors. Gomez, Gujarati, and Heckendorn (2012) state that a sense of belonging can mitigate feelings of anxiety and vulnerability students may feel as they speak in front of an audience of their peers in Spanish classrooms. Furthermore, they also state that a classroom community is characterized by trust, safety, respect and the creation of a safe space for sharing.

Different strategies of building community in the language classroom may include exploring narratives of students' identities that delve into the omnipresent sociolinguistic power structures in their lives (Lapayese, 2016), and using writing as a device for communication and connections (Gomez, Gujarati, & Heckendorn, 2012). And finally, introducing *play* into the classroom routine may give permission and incentive for students to develop their language skills along with their identities as speakers of the language. Paley (2004) suggests that fantasy play is one of the most important ways in which young children develop academic and social skills. Paley also argues that anything we add to the mix along with play further advances learning, for example, drawing, clay, books, music, games and dance. Yet Paley states that, "the ability to play is what opens gates to other pathways" (p. 72). Those pathways that play provides may prove to be transferable to students in high school language classrooms. I put this to the test by inviting my students to play outside together, sometimes it was frisbee and sometimes it was soccer. We laughed and connected in a different way, this allowed us to come back and ground our discussions about reading and writing in a more trusting way because we had taken the time to simply see each other's humanity through play.

I incorporated these strategies by having my students reflect and share through drawing, surveys, free-writes, class feedback—"What is going well?" "What could be better?"—end of semester reflections, and finally having them write their own personal narratives as language learners. I took my student work, words and attitudes and analyzed it as data. Throughout the semester we built community by celebrating birthdays, accomplishments, sharing food, playing soccer outside and, overall, just being around each other in important moments, like when we grieved and mourned together when one of our class members passed away that spring. It was heartbreaking, I cried with my students and they with me. The process looked different for each of us in the room and like many of the things that happen in my classroom with my students—they are not my stories to tell. They do not belong to me. Each person carried their own grief, brought in their own trauma and love and we grew both together and apart from the experience. We became what many students called family. I used that word, too, and meant it. We shared meals, music and written work that would be something that would make the other people in class proud of us. I participated in each assignment, read every chapter, engaged in seminar discussions, I also wrote poetry and the personal narratives that I asked my students to produce. For me, it was an extremely powerful way of teaching and learning.

My master's program work challenged me to listen intently to my students' needs. It gave me space and valor to create something unique and brand new. To this day, this work lights me up. It reminds me of what teaching is all about—teaching who we are and who our students are. As students and educators of color, we need so many layers of support to finally realize who we are. The solution to oppression, and the pathway to creating a welcoming space for immigrant and refugee students in schools, which are spaces that are systematically oppressive, cannot just be one thing (Love, 2020). It takes many things, but hopefully one of those things is something that fuels your passion as a teacher and has your students learn that their being is bigger than just themselves.

## 2018 New Mexico Teacher of the Year

Teaching awards are interesting, they are needed—teachers deserve recognition for their work and what would otherwise only live within the walls of their classrooms. One of the main drawbacks, in my opinion, is that they almost always alienate the teacher selected. It leaves colleagues feeling unseen, and underappreciated even as their coworker gets the recognition, we all need. Of course, teachers in general do not take part in their amazing craft and profession because of awards or recognition, on the contrary, they do it for the good of their community and their students. So many would argue they are not necessary. Yet, they exist.

Another interesting aspect of these awards is that they are also often large catalysts that change the trajectory of an educator's career—finally placing them in the rooms where their ideas can be exposed and, because of the title and platform, finally heard. After an award like State Teacher of the Year, many educators pursue work in politics and policy, their state unions, they become consultants for publishing companies, they become inspirational public speakers, get book deals (hey!). Of course, every educator's journey is different, many were already doing the aforementioned things and that was one of the many reasons they're nominated for their award.

My nomination and New Mexico Teacher of the Year award has humble beginnings. In the middle of my M.A. program when I was focusing on student growth and reflecting on my practice, my principal at the small charter school where I worked, talked to me about the nomination and application. As I understand it, this process varies widely from state to state, but they all mirror the national application closely which consists of five written, extensive essays ranging in topics from teacher needs, pedagogy and equity. I wrote my application and used a lot of my M.A. work as inspiration for what I know can be a successful learning community. I was then selected as a state finalist and was required to send in answers to a series of questions in polished videos that Su Hudson, the Film and Media teacher at my school, edited for me.

I was then surprised in my classroom by the State Secretary of Education, my administrators, my wife, my parents and sister, and even Mr. Kennedy! My science teacher from high school who had encouraged me to become a teacher. I could not believe it was happening, but I embraced the accolades and set off to become part of a great educator community amongst other state teachers of the year.

I had the opportunity of working with amazing educators like Leah and Mandy and later meeting Sarahí who are now writing this book with me. If impostor syndrome has ever been real for me, it has been around the accolades of this State Teacher of the Year title. I still struggle with it, but I remind myself that every year there is someone selected, so why not me? That became my mantra during the year. Somebody will give the keynote at that conference, why not me? Somebody will be asked to speak on issues of education with the legislative committee, why not me? The biggest *why not me* moment came right before the White House Ceremony for all State Teachers of the Year in May of 2018. The politics at the time were less than ideal, and immigrants had been constantly called rapists, criminals and "bad hombres" by the President of the United States. So, I remember vividly during breakfast one morning, I was pulled aside by Mandy and John Juravich, 2018, Ohio Teacher of the Year and National semi-finalist, and they said something along the lines of, "Ivonne, if you want to sit out from the White House Ceremony, we will do it with you, and there are others who will too. We've got your back." And I thought, somebody will be in the White House being celebrated for serving students and their families, why not me? And I said, "Um, of course I'm going!" and we did. This moment still means so much to me, that fellow members of my cohort were willing to stand in solidarity with me.

The morning of The White House Ceremony, I was nervous. I went for a walk with my wife and tried to center myself for the experience later that day. It was humid, which it never is here in Albuquerque, my skin felt clammy and my stomach felt strange. I put on the fancy dress and jacket I had purchased for the occasion. I had been so nervous for this experience for many weeks, I knew I would have to be in that room. I knew that my presence was political, and these thoughts were turning my stomach. So, I turned to my most powerful support system—my students. I wrote to them on Google Classroom. I told them I was nervous, I was nervous of being simply too much not what the people there think America should look like. And I said in my letter, "but you and I know what America looks like. It looks like you, it looks like me." The responses from my students came pouring in. They said they were proud, that they love and support me. I read their comments on the bus to the White House and I sat just a little taller. I knew it was going to be okay.

We arrived at the Eisenhower Executive Office Building where we were to be checked in and go through security and eventually walk over to the adjacent White House. When I checked in, there seemed to be an issue. They asked me to step aside. Other State Teacher of the Year and their spouses kept walking in without a problem, they were all being handed a security badge, perhaps green or blue, to wear visibly on their jackets. Finally, after what seemed like a long time, they allowed me to walk into a lobby where I was instructed to wait. I was then introduced to a security guard who would be my escort given my "restricted" status, I was given a pink badge that had the word *restricted* on it, and then I was guided to the room where the rest of my cohort was already seated for a panel talk including all four national teacher of the year finalists. Members from my cohort looked at me with concern, "everything okay?" they mouthed and whispered. I smiled, if anybody is going to be in the room wearing a restricted badge with a special security officer, why not me? I snapped a selfie wearing the restricted badge, it is still one of my favorite pictures from the day.

## Concluding Thoughts

My year as a state teacher of the year was life-changing and career altering as well. It propelled me onto a main stage where I could talk about my experiences as an immigrant, as a woman of color, as an English Language Learner, and eventually to use the power of my voice and story to advocate for immigrants like me, particularly children through the creation of Teachers Against Child Detention.

 ## Reflection Questions

1.  What do *your* students need, particularly immigrant and refugee students?
2.  How does your teaching pedagogy fulfill those needs?
3.  The adjustments that happened to the Spanish heritage learners curriculum in my school came after listening to students' needs and also listening to the silences that

were present. In what ways can you focus your listening to ensure you're serving your students well in your classroom?

4. Outside forces, like awards or class and racial privilege, can give teachers a powerful shield to stand behind and advocate for their students. What empowers you to speak up on behalf of your students?

## References

Carreira, M. (2007). Spanish-for-native-speaker matters: Narrowing the Latino achievement gap through Spanish language instruction. *Heritage Language Journal, 5*(1), 147–171.

Flores, G. M. (2011). Racialized tokens: Latina teachers negotiating, surviving and thriving in a white woman's profession. *Qualitative Sociology, 34*(1), 313–335.

Gomez, D., Gujarati, J., & Heckendorn, R. (2012). The orbital experience: Building community through communication and connections in high school Spanish classes. *American Secondary Education, 41*(1), 96–117.

hooks, b. (1994). *Teaching to Transgress: Education as the Practice of Freedom*. New York: Routledge.

Lapayese, Y. V. (2016). Identifying the cracks; that's where the light slips in: The narratives of Latina/o bilingual middle-class youth. *The CATESOL Journal, 28*(1), 161–174.

Leeman, J. (2005). Engaging critical pedagogy: Spanish for native speakers. *Foreign Language Annals, 38*(1), 35–45.

Love, B. L. (2020). *We Want to do More Than Survive: Abolitionist Teaching and the Pursuit of Educational Freedom*. Boston, MA: Beacon Press.

Mikulski, A. M. (2006). Accent-uating rules and relationships: Motivations, attitudes, and goals in a Spanish for native speakers class. *Foreign Language Annals, 39*(4), 660–682.

Nakkula, M. J., & Toshalis, E. (2016). *Understanding Youth: Adolescent Development for Educators*. Cambridge, MA: Harvard Education Press.

Paley, V. G. (2004). *A Child's Work: The Importance of Fantasy Play*. Chicago, IL: The University of Chicago Press.

Real Academia Española. http://www.rae.es/la-institucion

Schaps, E. (2003). Creating a school community. *Educational Leadership*, *60*(6), 31–33.

Valdés, G. (1978). *Code Switching and the Classroom Teacher*. Arlington, VA: Center for Applied Linguistics.

Vygotsky, L. S. (1980). *Mind in Society: The Development of Higher Mental Process*. Cambridge, MA: Harvard University Press.

# 3

# Advocacy Within and Beyond the Classroom

## Identity in our Classrooms

Circles of My Multicultural Self has been one of my favorite ways to get to know my students. The template and lesson can be found on edchange.org. The activity has students write their names in the center of a piece of paper, then explore each of the identities that make up their own self and write them in circles surrounding their name. They may list things like Latino, or athlete, brother, trans, Jewish, etc. Once that is complete, they think of a moment in which they were especially proud to be one of their identities, and a moment that was particularly painful to be one of their identities. They then think of a stereotype associated with one of their identities that they do not fit into and fill in the blanks for the sentence "I am (a/an) _____ but I am NOT (a/an) _____." For example, my typical go-to sentence is "I am an immigrant, but I am NOT a criminal." After thinking of their stories/moments and filling in their stereotype sentences, the group engages in active listening to each other's identities and stories.

It is of particular importance that the teacher partakes in reciprocal pedagogy and, also, shares their own identities, stories and stereotype sentences. An activity like this one requires a

DOI: 10.4324/9781003177333-5

safe space and community, and it is often more successful once students already know a little bit about each other. Identity is such a complex idea, one which we must keep unpacking through our lives.

I have engaged in the work of unpacking my identities as a first-generation college student, teacher, immigrant, queer, woman-of color, mother and wife. Every one of these walking together, all of the time, I have had to work really hard at being comfortable with the idea of bringing all of these things with me into all the spaces that I occupy. I am now an adult, and sometimes it is still uncomfortable, but necessary to be mindful about bringing all of me.

It is crucial that our classrooms are the spaces that affirm who students are, and we cannot affirm what we do not know. We cannot affirm what students leave outside of our classroom walls. So, we must invite them, ask them in, and learn about them and affirm their identities in a more than superficial way. This leads to an open space in which learning can flourish, in which learning is anchored to community and each other as members of said community.

A way in which my identity has shifted in the past decade is tied closely to my immigration status and the way I am literally allowed to move in the world. As an undocumented high school student, I was hesitant to imagine a future that may be too big and too unrealistic. As a deferred action for childhood arrivals (DACA) recipient, I was hesitant to be too optimistic—I knew that the immigration system was not fair and it may take away my safety just as easily as it granted it to me. And now, thanks to my dearest wife, Nadia, I am a U.S. Permanent Resident.

With my Resident Card, also known as a green card, I humorously received a pamphlet from the U.S. government titled "Welcome to the United States: A Guide for New Immigrants." After living in this country for more than half my life, I surely could have written the pamphlet myself. I found myself with newly found freedom, I could travel outside the country, my social security number is no longer flagged anytime I use it as it was when it was given to me under DACA. I now study for the citizenship test in the rare moments when I have spare time.

I wonder what it will feel like to be a U.S. citizen. I was amazed when my daughter was born and shortly after, we received her social security card in the mail, something I coveted for almost my entire life was mailed seemingly automatically to our beautiful baby girl.

I keep on refilling the circles in my head. Undocumented. DACAmented. Documented, for real. And, my heart aches a little bit. It aches for all of the past circles, for that 17-year-old young student who did not know what the world had in store for her. I wish I could go back and tell her. At the end of the day, as a teacher, I aim to spread that message of hope to my students. I can't go back and tell myself, but I can tell them every day: What you are makes you yourself, but yourself is always changing and that is a good thing.

## Teachers Against Child Detention—Beginning of Activism/Advocacy

I admire the people for whom activism and advocacy is a core part of their identity and those who seamlessly bring their passion into their lessons, teaching craft, and then connect that to the wonderful work already going on in their communities. Before my teaching award, my activism and critical work were done within the walls of my classroom. I had not done the work of activism in an outward way. I kept my advocacy centered around students who I worked with and their families. I admired from afar the advocacy groups on my university campus who were part of the Undocumented and Unafraid movement. For as long as I can remember, I had always lived in fear. It felt as if my DACA may be taken away at any moment. I kept my head down, did my job quietly and well, which many immigrants must do in order to survive. We do our work in silence and shadows, even when exceptionally, and only share our documentation status with those who must know or those we trust dearly.

Then, my State Teacher of the Year Award came and with it, a whole lot of media attention. Receiving the award put my personal story at the forefront of the media. I spoke at press conferences broadcasted by AP, I spoke at the NM Capitol Roundhouse, I attended the State of the Union with Senator Martin Heinrich along with over 50 other Dreamers invited by their Senators and Representatives to create a presence and keep on advocating for a path to citizenship for ourselves and our families. I am incredibly grateful for these experiences, it all felt like an incredible opportunity but also, in a hard to explain way, an emotional burden.

The platform I was given provided me a safe space to talk about the struggles of being a DACA recipient and to advocate for the immigrant community at large, from a personal perspective and also from the lens of an educator. I jumped in, with both feet, into the world of advocacy and activism. I had the great fortune of connecting with people whom I considered to be *legit activists*, the kind I had only dreamed of, but feared, being. My State Teacher of the Year platform gave me the safety I needed to speak up and advocate for all immigrants, but particularly unaccompanied minors arriving at our southern border.

The State Teacher of the Year program allowed me to connect with like-minded educators who are still my dear friends and now writing this book with me. I still remember the beginning of the conversations with Mandy when we decided we could use our platforms to speak up and try to move the needle when it came to attention and policy regarding the treatment of unaccompanied minors by U.S. Immigration and Customs Enforcement (ICE). It was in those conversations that the idea of a national network of teachers, equally outraged by the caging and imprisonment of children, was born.

Many State Teachers of the Year from our cohort were involved in the creation of Teachers Against Child Detention, Mandy also skillfully brought in a lot of her activist contacts from Washington state who then put us in contact with people already doing the work near the border. Groups such as Learning for Justice, Ysleta Teachers Association, Hope Border Institute, United We Dream, Texas State Teachers Association, Borderland Rainbow Center, Indivisible El Paso, TX, San Antonio Educators Association, Las Americas Immigrant Advocacy Center, El Paso Teachers Association and many more.

After many months of organizing, and collaborating with partners during long, weekly Zoom meetings (this was pre-pandemic and people were not using video conferencing quite as often as we do now), on Presidents' Day 2019 we hosted a Teach-In event at the San Jacinto Plaza in El Paso, TX. We had many teachers from all over the country attend the Teach-In and a lot of them taught lessons on immigration, from history to curriculum development. We taught on the plaza for over eight hours, while live-streaming the event. We were so fortunate to work with the powerhouse groups already doing amazing work who invited us in and gave us the space to speak out and join their efforts. We learned from the organizations that were present that many times ICE will release immigrants in the middle of the night in the very plaza where we stood, without money or resources. The groups working at the border provide basic items for these people, access to a phone, access to lawyers, but perhaps most importantly—they see them as people again. At the Teach-In, we heard teachers share the stories of their students, their journeys to America, we had teachers, like myself, share their own stories as immigrant children and now professionals in this country.

At the time of the event, it was the closest I had been to Mexico, to the border, in over 15 years. About ten years before that, my older sister had been detained in El Paso after trying to cross the border without documents. She was incarcerated for 14 days. She was only 18 years old at the time. I thought about the legacy the border has had on my family's history, my grandfather participating in the Braceros program of the 1940s and 1950s. I thought of my own parents making the decision to bring us over to this side. I could see the colorful buildings beyond the tall fence. It looked like I thought Mexico would look. I thought of all the young children being kept away from their families, much farther away from home than I had been when I was 12 and crossed the border myself. I felt overwhelmed by the sense of community that groups in El Paso provided us and continue to provide for immigrants in need at the border, but also, I was so inspired by the dozens of teachers who took the time to show up, to teach and to protest. It was a time of self-reflection for me, on the things that add up and allow us to build courage and speak out against what we know is wrong, or in support of what we know is right. What does it take to build courage? What do we need to finally say, that is enough and I need to do something? I know that for me, it was outrage and sadness after seeing the pictures and footage of young people being kept in tents, in cages, in the middle of the desert. I kept thinking, 15 years earlier, if timing and chance had failed me, that could have been me. In a prison without access to education and deprived of my humanity.

Activism comes in many shapes and forms. Sometimes, it is showing up at the protests, making our voices heard, or writing our representatives and sharing our stories with them that then they may share with the courts who make life-changing decisions for our lives. But perhaps some of the actions we take are smaller but equally powerful—designing a lesson around social justice in our classrooms; correcting someone when they mispronounce your name, again; having a conversation with one of our students about their future, the possibilities and the resources available to them regardless of immigration status. We must not discount all of the efforts we are already doing, while at the same time looking around to see which groups and causes, we may support with our work.

## TACD Albuquerque

A few months after our Teach-In, I was invited to be the keynote speaker for the commencement ceremony of the school where I was teaching at the time. It was a delight to connect to students in this way, I absolutely loved all the students graduating. It was during this speech that I mentioned my work with TACD, and the change the educators who had shown up had hoped to bring into the world. It was my great fortune that my now dear friend and colleague, Dair Obenshain, happened to be in the audience as her niece graduated.

After hearing of the work in that speech, Dair approached me and asked about TACD. I told her about the national network of teachers, and the way I hoped to bring that to a more local level, but I wasn't sure how that would work. It was through conversations with Dair that we decided to start TACD Albuquerque. It was as grassroots as it gets. Sitting at Dair's kitchen table we came up with a list of educators who might be interested in joining us. We composed a message, then a flier that we distributed on Facebook and email, and we invited educator friends to join us to the first meeting—hosted at Dair's house. For our first meeting in July of 2019, we had over 30 local educators there from many different schools, public, charter and private, all united to see what we could do as a group.

I was so excited to see the energy every single person at that meeting brought. Their love for the cause and their willingness to share their own stories and/or those of their students were mesmerizing to me. From that meeting, we had one of the educators volunteers to put together and manage a listserv for us. We created a network of local teachers all on the lookout for news, ordinances, or any other events that may be of interest to the other teachers on the list. It was through this system of community vigilance that we found out of efforts of a private, for-profit corporation to start a "group home" for undocumented children in Albuquerque. People on the listserv quickly joined other efforts being put together by other organizations: they called, they wrote, they spoke at neighborhood association meetings, and after all of these efforts the company retracted their proposal to host the group home in Albuquerque. To me, this is what our group is all about, creating networks of like-minded people who are willing to step in and create change in their own communities.

TACD Albuquerque grew. We hosted meetings at Dair's school, we invited old friends and made new ones. Along the way, Mirle Hernández, Louise Kahn and Francesca Blueher joined us in leading the group through education and actions. During the fall of 2019, TACD Albuquerque became a strong partner in the effort to divest our pensions in the NM Educational Retirement Board (NMERB) from private, for-profit prison stocks in our retirement portfolio. We found it insulting that our own money, from our hard-earned work as educators, was being invested in corporations that dehumanize people in New Mexico for a profit. We worked with other groups already advocating for the cause, we worked at educating ourselves in the issue, and we emailed and spoke to lawyers, investors and representatives on the board. We made our voices heard in NMERB meetings, we wrote op-eds, and members of TACD engaged in multiple conversations with members of the board about the moral and financial responsibility involved. The two stocks our retirement was formally invested in were GeoGroup and CoreCivic, these stocks were not doing well financially after losing support from most large banks. It made no sense for our money to be invested there, however the NMERB members insisted they did not have the power to divest due to an existing policy that prevented them from doing so. Finally in the fall of 2020, the NMERB voted to change said divestment policy, and even included wording that they will not invest in private, for-profit prison corporations in the future. It was a win, but it was exhausting, the work continues and now TACD and our activist partners such as FreeThemAll and New Mexico Dreamers Project continue the work to ensure that the NMERB does not just look at net profit of investments without taking into consideration that we are educators, and our students and families are valuable to us and we will not partake in anything that hurts them or our planet.

Furthermore, during this long campaign of divesting the NMERB from private, for-profit prisons, the COVID-19 pandemic ensued, and so we moved our meetings to Zoom, and our conversations to emails and text messages. We created a network that stayed in touch and supported each other through the reality that the pandemic brought to our classrooms and communities.

Through the birth and development of TACD Albuquerque, we have committed ourselves again and again to educating ourselves and other member teachers so that we may serve as resources for our immigrant students and their families. We have brought each other solidarity and support through the pandemic, even when our already difficult work seemed to become even harder. Another powerful insight provided by Dair, is that this work has led us to connect with many activist groups and this has served to educate us very quickly. For example, quite a few of our members went from thinking that prison abolition was a big idea that was not practical or that #DefundThePolice may not be the best campaign slogan as it could potentially alienate some people to now identifying themselves as prison and police abolitionists. Now that they understand how the school-to-prison pipeline is not an accident and the way this is connected to for-profit prisons that are tied to ICE and the way we treat immigrants and refugees in this country. Being able to work more and more online due to the pandemic gave us the opportunity to get directly in touch with many other activists and community leaders we previously had not worked with. It has made us more knowledgeable and better able to serve our students and families.

## Concluding Thoughts

It is by being part of groups like TACD Albuquerque that my sense of self and hope return each time I reflect on our work, the work that we have done and the work we will do. I had someone ask me once how we measure success. That's the interesting thing about community activism, the success of the work keeps on leading us to new work. I am so proud of what we have created here in Albuquerque, and I know we will keep on reaching new heights as we continue our work together as educators.

## Strategies for Starting Your own Local TACD Chapter or Organization

1. Think about people you know that would be willing to join your efforts.
2. Make a list of national or local organizations that are already doing work that you can join.
3. Define your purpose. For example, our TACD national purpose was to educate others and bring about large

policy changes. For TACD here in Albuquerque, our purpose is to keep educating ourselves and other teachers so we're prepared to serve our students. We are also working to bring policy change—like our efforts to divest ERB from private for-profit prisons.

4. Keep in mind that this is exhausting but rewarding work. Lean on your community. They'll have your back.

Part 2

# Using Literacy to Create a Welcoming Environment for Refugee and Immigrant Students

*By Leah Juelke*

# 4

# Sheltered Instruction

It was ten o'clock in the morning, which meant it was time to stop working. I found myself sitting outside with five Tanzanian teachers, eating mandazi and drinking tea. When I first was told that we had a break in the morning, I looked at it as a time to run to the bathroom and then to continue to work. After the second call to break, the head teacher came to where I was working and told me it was break time again. I thought this was a little peculiar and brushed it off as maybe he thought I didn't hear them. I nodded, and he just stared at me. It was clear that he wanted me to go with him. So, I awkwardly got up and followed him. He led me to an outdoor area where the teachers were sitting and chatting. Apparently, a mid-morning break for a teacher in Tanzania is not the same as what I was used to in America. Working through a break there was unheard of and not something they expected teachers to do. The communal sharing of fried bread and tea was a welcomed difference from the American teachers' work through a pile of emails and a stack of grading "break."

I had traveled to Arusha, Tanzania with my colleague, Cindy Benson, to train Tanzanian teachers in the Sheltered Instruction Observation Protocol (SIOP) Model. The Tanzanian government had recently announced that all high school classes would be taught in English from that year forward and teachers were looking for strategies to facilitate the change. An educational organization called Mwangaza brought teachers to the organization every summer to give a multitude of professional

DOI: 10.4324/9781003177333-7

development opportunities to their staff. In 2015, I won a grant through Fund for Teachers to go to Tanzania and South Africa to immerse myself in the culture and learn about Africa. The premise was to get a better understanding of my East African students and their school systems, as well as to collaborate with Tanzanian and South African teachers. In addition, my experiences teaching at a boarding school in Taiwan, a private school in Ecuador, a rural school in Costa Rica and a boarding school in China, gave me a unique perspective and understanding of the ever so varying educational experiences that students around the world have. These experiences made me start questioning my assumptions about my students' education. Consequently, the dialogue that took place due to my past experiences allowed me to connect with my students on a deeper level upon return.

English Learner (EL) teachers need to be able to step out of their comfort zones and step into their students' shoes. The more I learned about my students' backgrounds and their lives, the more I connected with them. This fostered a sense of trust and understanding, which led to my students feeling like they belonged in my class. When students have trust, understanding and a sense of belonging, it opens them up to focus on their own learning.

My official title is English Learner English teacher, although my students call me "Ms. J" or "Mama J." I work in one of the largest school districts in the state of North Dakota, which also features one of the largest and most comprehensive EL programs within the state. The program currently serves over 900 EL students among its 23 schools. Students come from over 20 different nations and speak a wide range of languages. Our city is known as a resettlement city, therefore the majority of my students are refugees. They come from refugee camps and war-torn countries, have interrupted formal education, trauma and little to no English fluency. Historically, my city has a predominantly White population. It was only in the late 1990s that the community started seeing an influx of refugees and immigrants.

As a student who graduated from the same school in 2001, I can attest that the school did not have many students of diverse backgrounds. During that time, the school was composed of 95% White U.S. born students. Today, that number is around 67%.

The diversity of the population has continued to grow at a rapid pace due to the low unemployment rate.

Almost all of my current students live well below the poverty line. There are over 900 students enrolled at the high school and 27.5% of the school population receives free or reduced lunch. As of the 2020–2021 school year, 67% of the school population identifies as White, 13.9% as Black, 6.3% as Asian, 5.3% as Hispanic, 4.1% Native American and 2.5% as other (About Us / Enrollment Data, n.d.). I teach a range of classes including EL English levels 1–4.

### Proficiency Levels from World-Class Instructional Design and Assessment (WIDA)

♦ 1: Entering: Knows and uses minimal social language and minimal academic language with visual and graphic support.

♦ 2: Emerging: Knows and uses some social English and general academic language with visual and graphic support.

♦ 3: Developing: Knows and uses social English and some specific academic language with visual and graphic support.

♦ 4: Expanding: Knows and uses social English and some technical academic language.

♦ 5: Bridging: Knows and uses social English and academic language working with grade-level material.

♦ 6: Reaching: Knows and uses social and academic language at the highest level measured by this test.

(WIDA, 2019)

I teach Intro to English, communications and a class that partners mentor students born in the U.S. with New American students, called Partnership for New Americans. Students whose native language is not English, take the state's English proficiency screener, the ACCESS Test.

Each of the six EL teachers also takes on the role of a case manager. We equally divide up the EL student roster to create caseloads. It is the responsibility of each teacher to create an Individualized Learning Plan (ILP) for the students on their roster. The additional duties of a case manager include attending academic or behavioral meetings, dealing with schedule changes, bussing concerns, attendance concerns and being a liaison between the school and home or the school and the EL social worker.

The EL classes are taught using Sheltered Instruction. This practice has been around since the 1980s (Freeman, D. & Freeman, Y., 1988). Although some aspects have changed, the main premise remains the same. Sheltered Instruction is a method that ensures that EL students' content and language needs must be met within their core classes. In the past, EL students were entirely separated from the mainstream students, but today students are only separated for their core classes and then take the rest of their classes alongside mainstream students. I have found that EL students prefer this structure because when in a sheltered classroom environment, they feel less intimidated when they are surrounded by students they can relate to, who are at similar English levels. They also enjoy making new friends and challenging themselves by taking electives with the rest of the student body. Our school invested in Career and Technical Education paraprofessionals, so there is extra help for them within elective classes such as sewing, auto, cooking, woods and digital photo. This was a tremendous help for our students and helped them gain more confidence in their skills. Does your school have these kinds of supports?

Along with content objectives, the teacher also incorporates English language objectives into their class. The four core classes are taught by highly qualified teachers, who are certified in both their content and in EL. Students attend these core classes exclusively with EL students and attend other classes with the rest of the student body (Freeman, D. & Freeman, Y., 1988).

## Sheltered English Instruction

Within the core EL classes, teachers use the SIOP Model. This model infuses aspects of language into the core content curriculum. Language objectives and content objectives are both integrated into the curriculum to facilitate age-appropriate language learning (Echevarria, Vogt, & Short, 2016). This model is especially important when teaching EL high school students, making content more accessible to them.

The SIOP Model is made up of eight components:

- ◆ Lesson Preparation
- ◆ Building Background
- ◆ Comprehensible Input
- ◆ Strategies
- ◆ Interaction
- ◆ Practice/Application
- ◆ Lesson Delivery
- ◆ Review & Assessment

A multitude of research favors the use of the SIOP Model for EL students. When teachers are trained to implement the model effectively, student language and academic gains are vast (*Center for Applied Linguistics*, 2018).

In 2014, our district high school EL department, consisting of myself and nine other EL teachers, sought to overhaul our level 1 intro class curriculum. The purpose of this intense curriculum writing was to align all level 1 intro classes with the same language objectives. The Intro to English, Intro to Science, Intro to Social Studies and Math 2 courses were all carefully analyzed, and existing language objectives were shifted to align with each other. Using our EL English text as the model, we organized language objectives to be taught concurrently during the year. When I would be teaching present progressive verbs in October, students would also be practicing those verbs in Science, Social Studies and Math, using the content of those classes as a vehicle for further practice. Students seemed to move through intro units faster than previous years, due to increased exposure to the same language concepts within each class. I noticed that my Intro to English class spent less time on certain grammatical concepts for each chapter than previous years. Students would comment, "Pronouns again? We already did this in science today!" They were recognizing that all of their core teachers were focusing on the same language concepts at the same time. I also saw students become more comfortable with school in general. Students knew what to expect and realized that their core teachers worked together.

One day, right before winter break, a sophomore boy came early to my class. I had a prep period right before and was working on grading at my desk when he enthusiastically swung my classroom door open. "Mrs. J! I have question. Homework?" he said in broken English. I smiled. He came toward my desk, while shuffling through his backpack. He took out two worksheets and asked me which one was English. Both worksheets focused on identifying plural nouns, but one used vocabulary from physical science and the other used vocabulary from our English class. I explained to him that both science and English learn the same grammar. He smiled. "That is so easy!" He told me he thought he had lost his science work, since both worksheets looked like English and last year his other classes didn't do English "like that." I explained to him that it was something new we were doing and he smiled and said that it was "easy when all the classes do the same." After that day, this student made a point of interrupting my prep hour, almost daily, to show me the worksheets from the other classes that "looked like English" and "were so easy now." Students would also comment that they "already learned this" in another class when I would introduce new concepts. I let them in on the secret that, yes, indeed, I did know that because I helped create the curriculum integration. Students liked the idea of their teachers working together as a team to make it "easier" for them. The consistency of the English language skills being taught in their core classes gave them a sense of structure and understanding. When districts adopt such integrative and aligned practices, it demonstrates their understanding of the diverse EL populations within their community, and in turn, fosters a welcoming environment. What strategies are used in your district to teach EL students?

## A Community Approach

It happened on my birthday, the same day that I stayed home from work, comforting my daughter, who was sick with the flu. Around noon, my daughter finally went down for a nap and I casually checked my school email. As soon as I did, my heart dropped. A student had drowned in the school pool during gym class. It was not just any student, but one of my EL students, I was devastated. Throughout this section, I will discuss what happened to this student and how it illustrates the huge strides my district and community took in serving EL populations.

Providing adequate and equitable services to the growing population of refugees with limited English proficiency has been a challenge for our community. Oftentimes, inequities occur within our EL population. Learning disabilities go undiagnosed because of low language ability and the age of the student. Parental involvement is limited since parents often feel ashamed that they don't speak English and have limited transportation. Since many families cannot afford cars, winter becomes a dangerous time due to the extreme temperatures. Some also struggle with abuse and violence due to the difficult transition, Post Traumatic Stress Disorder (PTSD) and traditional cultural practices. Many of my students come from very remote locations throughout Africa, Asia and the Middle East. It is common for them to start high school with little or severely interrupted formal education. It is also common for students to arrive and only speak a certain dialect of a language, making it difficult for them to communicate with our translators. This was the case with *Kenny. He spoke an African dialect that only one translator could somewhat understand. Kenny was an 18-year-old from the Democratic Republic of Congo in central Africa.

Kenny and his 20-year-old brother, *Carl, were both in my Intro to English class. Students are allowed to attend traditional high school classes until they turn 21 years old, after which, they are able to enroll in adult education or get their GED (test for general education development) at the alternative high school. If there are transcripts or knowledge of previous education, those factors are also taken into account when placing students into classes. Since the brothers came with no transcripts, and scored a 1, in the low range of the ACCESS screener test, they were placed into EL Intro classes. Their schedules were almost identical. Due to the integrative nature of the intro classes, they benefited greatly from the infusion of additional language skills within content classes.

Kenny loved wearing his baseball cap that he acquired during his years in the refugee camp. It reminded him of his childhood friends and warmer weather. He told me once that he could still smell the dust from the camp on the cap, and for him, that was a familiar and comforting smell.

I remember one day when class was just about to start, the principal stopped in my room, and without missing a beat, he walked over to Kenny and told him to take off his cap. Kenny was confused and eventually, he figured out what the principal was trying to tell him. The principal didn't know that Kenny wasn't blatantly disregarding the rules and didn't have a clear understanding of English, hence could not read the rules or syllabus. Kenny did not understand why he couldn't wear his cap in school. In his school in Congo, he couldn't wear a cap either, but he was under the impression that in America, you could do whatever you wanted to. "Just like the American movies," he told me once. Many of my students came to school in the U.S., thinking it was going to be like what they saw on television.

As with all newcomers, teachers and other students, Kenny and Carl relied heavily on gestures, repetition and Google translator. Eventually, the brothers' skills grew due to their motivation to learn and to fit in. Within six months, Kenny and Carl could have short conversations and were able to express themselves with limited simple tense verbs. They had many new experiences, and participated in sports and activities that they had only ever heard of before.

Like many of our refugee students, swim lessons weren't a privilege that they grew up with. Neither Kenny nor Carl knew how to swim. Many even had fear of the water, due to incidents in their native countries, watching their friends drowning or being swept away in the currents of the rivers in which they washed clothes or bathed.

On the morning of February 18, 2014, five months after arriving in the United States, Kenny headed to his P.E. class. The class had a group of EL students within the same class since their schedules aligned. They were swimming in class and on this day, they were doing swim tests. Kenny and his brothers had previously told their friends that they were scared to swim, but they participated anyway. There were two adults in the pool that day, one P.E. teacher, who was also a certified lifeguard and a student teacher.

At home, I started to read through the long email chain of messages. The first notified everyone that there was an incident happening in P.E. class. It is routine for the administration to send out an email if there are student situations that would warrant a lockdown of a certain part of the school. I thought nothing of it and read on. The next message asked for help to keep students out of the area. The next explained that emergency services were on the scene. Another message, sent to EL teachers, asked if any one of us were free to go to the pool. If there were any issues with an EL student, academic or behavioral, an EL teacher was always contacted.

Having a sheltered instruction model in place helped create a collaborative problem-solving environment, so our EL students wouldn't fall through the cracks. So, that day, one of the teachers responded that she was on the way. Frantically, I messaged my colleague to find out what had happened, since I was reading the emails an hour later. She informed me that Kenny had been pulled from the pool during gym class and the teacher had done Cardiopulmonary Resuscitation (CPR) on him. The ambulance took him to the hospital and that was all that she knew.

Kenny ended up on life support. Students who witnessed the incident explained how they saw Kenny in the deep end of the pool, while the others were in the shallow end of the pool testing on skills or in the bleachers. They recall the teacher telling them to stay out of the deep water if they were not strong swimmers. Students recounted that one moment they saw Kenny hanging onto the side of the pool and then the next he wasn't. He was pulled out from the deep end of the pool by the student teacher, who started CPR immediately.

Imagine being a refugee, who just came to this country months or weeks before this incident and watching your friend's lifeless body being pulled from the pool and having no way to communicate what you saw or how you felt about it. That was the reality for many of those EL students in that gym class that day.

Due to the sheltered instruction structure of classes, students had the same core teachers and often traveled with each other to their core classes. The structure creates a type of camaraderie amongst the students. Even though they speak different languages and come from different countries, they are all learning at a similar level and generously help each other. Each teacher was able to talk with the students during class about how they were feeling.

I had students come and eat lunch with me in my classroom and some who would stay after school just to talk. "I will never go in a pool again," one of my students told me at lunch one day. The school closed the pool, but some students still skipped gym class after the accident. They were traumatized. I felt it too. You could see from the worried looks on their faces when they came into class, and their constant questions about Kenny. "Ms. J, will he be good? Will he live?" I had no answers for them. All I could do was to create a safe space for them to ask questions and to process what was happening.

The students had four core EL teachers who understood what they were going through. We knew that these students were a close group of friends and we changed our lesson plans when needed, so that any questions or issues that arose could be addressed. I remember one day when I was getting ready to teach about adjectives and I looked over and saw a student with her head on her desk.

"Are you okay?" I asked her softly.

"Sad," she said as she lifted her head and looked at me.

Another student said, "She think school no safe."

My heart sank. I stopped the lesson and had the students circle their desks around. They talked and I listened. These students had been through so much, recently arriving in the U.S. and now this tragedy had shaken their faith and trust in their new community. The school counselors were also available for our students, but due to the language barrier, most of the students felt more comfortable talking to their EL teachers, the ones who knew them better and could always figure out what they were trying to say.

A week later, a few EL teachers, the EL social worker and I were able to visit Kenny in the hospital. Since we have a close knit EL department, due to our sheltered instruction structure, we were able to work with the EL social worker and organize a visit. Kenny had been put on a ventilator and into a drug-induced coma to help his lungs heal. Kenny's mother wasn't there when we arrived. She was home resting. She was older and had health problems of her own. Before coming to America, she had survived a house fire in Africa that killed five of her eight children. Thinking of her losing another child after such a tragedy broke my heart.

I remember walking into his hospital room, seeing him lying there unconscious with tubes down his throat. I saw a whiteboard that had some phrases translated from his native language into English for the doctors to practice saying. The family was only able to find one person in the whole area who spoke his native language to help interpret, but he wasn't always available. Due to that, communication among all parties during this critical time was very difficult. The interpreter had told the doctors it would be better for them to use familiar phrases in Kenny's language to talk to him.

Kenny was still heavily sedated up until a day before we visited. That day, Kenny's brother reported that he had opened his eyes for the first time. His eyes seemed to be following people around the room. The doctors became optimistic and said that he was slowly improving and that they might be able to take the breathing tube out within days.

I watched as Carl took a CD from his bag and put it in the CD player near the bed. A calm song with lyrics in his native language played by the speaker. "This one, his favorite," he told us. My eyes filled with tears, but I tried to remain strong and fight them back. We presented the many cards to Carl that his classmates had made for Kenny. A huge smile spread across his face and he said "Kenny will like."

Three days later, Kenny died. I remember attending his funeral with my colleagues and my students. As a teacher, I wanted to remain strong for my students and not let them see me cry, but the moment that I entered the church, and saw a group of my students and his mother standing by the casket, it was impossible to hold back the tears. Losing a student breaks you in a way that is indescribable.

During the two weeks that he was in the hospital and after his death, Kenny's family, the school and community members had become frustrated with the language and culture barriers. The services that were already in place by the refugee resettlement agency in town, our SIOP structure and our school's very own EL social worker were the keys that helped open the door for collaboration, understanding and healing. But for some, it just wasn't enough. It was hard for Kenny's family to understand exactly what happened in that pool that day. They had so much respect for teachers and school. It was supposed to be a safe place. Imagine escaping a war-torn country, living in a refugee camp for years, surviving a fatal fire that took the lives of your children, moving across the world to a place where you thought your family would finally be safe, only for tragedy to strike yet again.

Due to the lack of native speakers of Kenny's language, the process of collaboration during such trauma was very difficult. A year and a half later, Kenny's mother had succumbed to cancer at age 60 and his older brother was still trying to make sense of his new reality. Not understanding his legal rights until too late, Kenny's older brother looked to take legal action against the school, but the statute of limitations had expired. This strained the relationships of many refugees and immigrants in the area and others in the community. In the end, Kenny's death was ruled an accident.

Even though we had many districts and community-wide initiatives targeting our EL populations, it was clear from this tragedy that more needed to be done. For the safety of all, changes were made to pool use, district-wide, and it was decided that a certified lifeguard was to be present, in addition to the teacher during swimming in P.E. class. Our superintendent was deeply touched by this tragedy and he made it his mission to make cultural diversity awareness and education a priority within our schools and community. My principals became more intentional with their EL focused professional development opportunities and continued to give the EL teachers the autonomy to make decisions as professionals. An additional EL social worker was added to our staff and I helped to conduct multiple professional development training sessions, educating school staff on who our EL students are and how to support them. A position called the community liaison police officer was created in 2008 to support the growing number of refugee and immigrant families arriving in our community. Another position called a Community Trust Officer was also added and works in conjunction with the liaison to help build community partnerships.

I noticed more initiatives being launched to collaborate and educate after Kenny's death. There were free community swimming lessons offered to youth in the community. Additionally, community block parties and parties in the park were among some of the initiatives to help create a more welcoming community. In 2017 and 2018, our police department partnered with billboard artists DPB and Crew to create music videos to advocate for unity and understanding. A couple of local officers are talented rappers and were inspired to use music to help spread their message. They went to local schools and included refugee and immigrant students, among others, dancing in their music videos. The officers and DPB and Crew also visited schools and presented their motivational videos and gave presentations during all school assemblies.

I remember watching the rap video for the first time on Youtube. It was heart-warming to see some of my EL students and their parents dancing and smiling in the video. My students, who are often left out due to the barriers they face, felt like they were a part of something bigger, and they were. (Link to video— https://www.youtube.com/watch?v=gTXtUefEVJo)

Our district created a Diversity, Inclusion, and Equity Statement that, in part, reads: "We will achieve excellence by educating and empowering all students to succeed. We will honor the uniqueness of each individual, embrace diverse backgrounds, values, and points of view to help build a strong, inclusive school community; and prepare students as active agents of their multicultural society."

The statement also mentions that: "Education is better where schools are composed of students, teachers and families drawn from diverse socioeconomic backgrounds, cultures, "races"/ ethnicities, religions and sexual orientations. Yet a diverse school community alone is not enough. Inclusion matters...we seek to make our diversity one of our strongest assets." (Equity & Inclusion / Equity Action Plan, n.d.)

In addition, our school is in the process of creating an Equity Action Plan (Figure 4.1). This plan is modeled after a variety of different districts, including the Fridley Public Schools district in Minnesota. The plan discusses what equity looks and feels like. It is important to address such issues when looking to create a welcoming community for diverse populations. The plan is said to help the district "grow, embrace change, and model the practice of personal reflection and professional collective accountability" (Equity & Inclusion / Equity Action Plan, n.d.).

It is one thing to pen a mission statement or plan, but quite another to actually take action. In 2020, the school system hired a full-time Director of Equity and Inclusion to work within the district. The district is open to learning more about how to better itself when it comes to integrating a comprehensive and cohesive equity plan into our school culture.

---

**DISTRICT EQUITY ACTION PLAN STATEMENTS**

We believe educational equity looks like:

- Authentic, caring relationships with and among students, staff, and families
- Culturally inclusive pedagogy
- High expectations for each student to meet grade level expectations and experience "on time" graduation with his/her/their 9th grade cohort
- Parity in enrollment in advanced courses
- Reflective and adaptive curriculum
- Welcoming and safe school environments
- System-wide outcomes that contribute to a more just Fargo community and world.

We believe educational equity feels like we can each say:

- I am seen for my strengths and contributions
- I am respected for who I am
- My voice is heard and appreciated
- I feel cared about and I care about others
- I see myself represented positively in my school's curriculum
- I feel comfortable and welcomed at school
- I am academically confident and challenged
- I am empowered to achieve my goals, my dreams, and my full potential
- I see my place and responsibility in creating a more just society

---

**FIGURE 4.1** Fargo Public School's District Equity Action Plan Statements
https://www.fargo.k12.nd.us/Page/2574

Kenny's death was a tragedy, but it was also a catalyst for many changes within the school district. Every child deserves a high-quality education within an accommodating environment, no matter where they were born. Educators and administrators need to be open to change and be willing to truly listen to their students. What policies could be changed to better the relationships that EL families and students have with the school or district? How is your district addressing equity and diversity? If you have concerns, reach out to leadership. Don't wait until a tragedy strikes to find out.

## It Takes a Village

When I first started in the district, our EL director, Vonnie, managed the EL program, which spanned about 23 schools. She did the job of three people, managing the many tasks that were asked of her. Vonnie had a kind nature and had been working with EL students for almost her whole career. You could tell in one conversation with Vonnie that her passion was to help people. She loved working with refugee and immigrant families, and she was good at what she did. Her warm smile was inviting and she radiated joy. She brought all of the EL teachers in the district together for monthly meetings. There was never a meeting that didn't have snacks and coffee. At every meeting, Vonnie would start by asking the staff about any celebrations that they wanted to share. One of the best things about Vonnie was that no matter when an EL family would come to her office, she always made time for them. She would sit down with each family and ask them a variety of important questions to get to know them. She would write down the answers and use the information to determine which services the family needed. She would pass on vital information to teachers so that they would better understand the backgrounds of the incoming EL students and their families.

I would mention Vonnie's name to my students, their faces would light up and they would refer to her as the "sweet grandma" that they met when they first arrived. When Vonnie announced her retirement in 2016, I was crushed because no one could ever replace such an amazing director. I learned from Vonnie that it is important for an EL director to foster a sense of community amongst her staff and to create a loving and welcoming environment for our EL families, from the moment they walk in the door.

I often tell people that the secret to success for our EL program not only lies in the sheltered instruction model and a dedicated director, but also in utilizing the positions of the EL social worker and the bilingual paraprofessional. It really does take a village. These professionals are the line of communication between home and school for our EL families.

Our EL social worker was assigned to our high school and various other schools within our district. When I met her my first year at the school, in 2013, her passion to work with our EL families radiated from the smile on her face. Our six-person sheltered instruction model EL department would have weekly lunch meetings with her to discuss student concerns. She would tell us information related to students with whom we worked. Since her position allowed her to do home visits and connect with EL families outside of school, her information and perspective were often the missing links that we needed to better understand our students. Teachers would also share information with her regarding behaviors or academic progress of students so that she could help connect with the families. Oftentimes, it felt like we were putting pieces of a puzzle together when working with her. Each piece that we fit together, was another piece of information that would help us better understand and serve our students.

Our social worker was outstanding at her job and our refugee and immigrant family population welcomed her into their homes and their hearts. One day when our lunch meeting was running a little late, a student walked into my classroom where we were having the meeting, and looked a little embarrassed, realizing that she interrupted. But she quickly got over that and yelled, "I miss you!" Another student from the hall heard and rushed in. "What? She's here? What are you doing?" They rushed to give her a big hug. This was a normal reaction from my high school EL students when they saw the EL social worker. The sense of trust and community was great.

To better understand our refugee families from Nepal, she traveled to Nepal in 2013 for a couple of weeks. Her dedication to her job earned her the title of District Staff Member of the Year. Every school district that serves EL students should have a specific social worker assigned to them. This has proven to be a much-needed lifeline for our EL families.

Over the years, it was clear that our EL social workers were spread thin, due to our growing EL population, and that the amount of help our EL students and families needed surpassed what our district had to offer. Luckily, an additional EL social worker position was added and our district now had three to work between the 23 schools. Eventually, the district made a change and we no longer had social workers designated solely to EL populations. This new structure broke our lifeline to our EL families and the services that we were able to provide. The trust that was built between our families and social workers was now gone and it was more difficult for social workers to address the concerns of our EL families, since there was a new referral process. With this process, students were referred to one of the social workers and added to the list. Since the social workers now served the general populations as well, the lists were long and often students' needs went unmet. Schools need to be able to provide services to EL families that breed trust and understanding. A designated EL social worker, outreach professional or liaison is essential to creating a welcoming community for EL families.

Bilingual Paraprofessionals are an integral part of serving EL students and families. Since I work in a school with students from over 20 different countries, it is impossible to get a paraprofessional that speaks each language. It was possible though to hire a paraprofessional who spoke the language from one of our larger EL student populations.

Damber Subba came to the U.S. as a refugee from Nepal, where a large portion of our students came from. He was forced to leave his country of Bhutan and live in the Nepali refugee camps, just as the parents of our Nepali students had. Damber was a teacher and administrator in Nepal and in the refugee camp, but when he came to the United States, none of his credentials transferred. So, he took a position as a paraprofessional. Damber is a kind soul and everyone loves him. He is soft-spoken and is always ready to help anyone. He spends his days following our low-level students throughout their schedule and aiding wherever needed. Damber translates instructions for students if needed, interprets for parent conferences and makes phone calls to Nepali parents.

One of my favorite times of the year is when Damber presents to the students. He talks about how the Bhutanese people were forced to leave Bhutan and his story of how he ended up fleeing the country in the middle of a deadly massacre. So many of our students have no idea why their parents ended up in refugee camps since they often won't talk about it. Damber has helped us to understand the Nepali culture on a deeper level. He regularly invites the teachers to cultural festivals and gives us insight into Nepali families and their parenting practices.

Damber also owns a local Asian market in town and he is an accomplished singer and songwriter. He is a big name in the US Nepali music community and has put out an album of Nepali songs. In addition, he is involved in a Nepali community group that provides help to those families with Coronavirus and those who are unaware of what to do or where to get supplies, testing or vaccines. The teachers often say that they wish there were multiple "Dambers" in our school. Every school, certainly, needs a Damber.

## Concluding Thoughts

Creating a welcoming environment for EL students and their families is multifaceted. It is important to have a strategic plan that addresses the specific needs of the students. Incorporating sheltered instruction and the corresponding strategies within an EL student's day sets them up for success and creates a foundation for growth. Infusing core curriculums with language rich content can facilitate learning. It is also important to evaluate your services and practices to ensure that they are equitable and adequate for your EL populations. Connecting with students and families is the key to knowing what services are needed. Educators need to be willing to learn about where their students came from and about their educational background. EL specific social workers and bilingual paraprofessionals are an essential link, connecting families with the school. Districts also need to be flexible and willing to change policies and programs, if they are not truly serving those in need. To have a successful EL program, it really does take a village. I know that somewhere, Kenny is smiling down at our village, knowing that he mattered. He made a difference.

 ## Reflection Questions

1. What kind of instructional supports does your school have for EL students?
2. Does your school have EL specific social workers? Bilingual paraprofessionals?
3. Think of an EL student that you have worked with. What is one thing you could do for that student to facilitate the transition to a new school?
4. Have you ever done a home visit?

*Names in this chapter have been changed.

## References

About Us / Enrollment Data. (n.d.). www.fargo.k12.wd.us. Retrieved November 12, 2021, from https://www.fargo.k12.nd.us/Page/365

*Center for Applied Linguistics.* (2018). Center for Applied Linguistics. Retrieved November 12, 2021, from https://www.cal.org/siop/research/

Echevarria, J., Vogt, M., & Short, D.J. (2016). *Making Content Comprehensible for English Learners.* Pearson.

Equity & Inclusion / Equity Action Plan. (n.d.). www.fargo.k12.nd.us. Retrieved November 12, 2021, from https://www.fargo.k12.nd.us/Page/2574

Freeman, D., & Freeman, Y. (1988). *Sheltered English Instruction.* (ED301070). ERIC. Retrieved November 12, 2021, from https://eric.ed.gov/?id=ED301070

WIDA. (2019). *WIDA.* Wisc.edu. https://wida.wisc.edu/

# 5

# Journey to America

"We started running and in the blink of an eye, we heard a gunshot and we all stopped. We looked back, and it was my dad. He had been shot. My older sister and I went back to see if he was still breathing. My father started talking to us, then suddenly one of the aggressive soldiers came and pushed us away from my dad. He poured gas on his body and lit him on fire right in front of us as we all cried. My father's body eventually turned to ash. There was nothing more left for us to do but to bury the ash. I was eight years old." Aline Uwase paused and wiped a tear from her eye and continued to read her story from the Journey to America book, which includes her story along with those of her classmates. When she was done, she lifted her head and addressed the panel of legislators in front of her.

"I want to say that I am here in this country because of the horrible crimes against my family. I am not here just to have fun. I am here to pursue my dream. I am here to make my parents proud. I am here to make the Americans proud. I have a job and I go to school. Now, I am a published author. I can help someone. At least now, I can motivate someone. I can be someone's mentor. People like me are not bad people, just because we are refugees. People like me are making your communities great. Please, I ask you not to pass this proposal."

DOI: 10.4324/9781003177333-8

There were smiles and nods from the large group of supporters behind Aline as she took her seat. Using stories they wrote for our Journey to America Project, Aline and two of her classmates testified at the state capitol against the proposal to limit refugee resettlement in North Dakota. The students had listened all morning as people belittled and chastised refugees and their resettlement in the community. In the end, the legislatures did not go forward with the measure. This is the kind of empowerment, engagement and empathy that I was hoping to teach students when I started the Journey to America project. I never imagined that it would have such a huge impact on myself, my students or the surrounding community.

During my first year working at my school, I noticed that there was a unit on narrative stories in the curriculum. Since all of my students were either refugees or immigrants, I had them write about their experiences coming to the United States. Many shared common experiences, whether it was living in a refugee camp, going on a plane or seeing snow for the first time in their lives. Once they started to brainstorm some ideas and write out a timeline of their lives, they seemed excited to share their common experiences.

"My mom was so scared of those moving stairs in the airport!" one student remarked.

"So was I! I remember falling on the stairs with my suitcase. It was so embarrassing," another student chimed in.

"My parents thought you had to pay to use the moving stairs, so we had to walk on the normal stairs," a third student remarked. I smiled as I listened to their excitement as they found similarities amongst themselves. Making these connections with each other are important for EL students. Many students feel lonely and do not have anyone to talk to about their feelings when they arrive in the United States. Being able to talk about their experiences and how they felt helps the students understand that they are not alone and others are going through similar experiences.

After reading the first drafts of stories, which at the time were simply a part of a class assignment, I was amazed at how much I learned about my students and how honest and heartbreaking their stories were. One student talked about how he had never been to school until he came to the U.S. at the age of 15. This student was now 17 years old. None of his teachers knew about his lack of education, but this new information made so much sense. This student wasn't progressing as fast as the other students and had issues with behavior and difficulty mastering certain skills. If someone is not literate in their native language and has never been to school, then clearly there would be some issues. The majority of my students and their families come to the U.S. with little ability to communicate in English, so important details, like schooling and academic skills were often not disclosed. I find out so much about each student, just sitting with them, helping them brainstorm for their stories.

> "So, you came here with your grandma and who else?" I asked *Aria.
> "Um. A baby girl," Aria said.
> "Oh, like your sister?" I asked.
> "No, like my daughter," Aria said as she looked up at my face, waiting for my reaction.

I tried not to look surprised, but I excitedly blurted out, "Oh really? How old is she? Do you have a picture?"

I wasn't quite sure how to react in that situation. At that time, I hadn't known many students who had children of their own, and if they did, I assumed I would have known at the beginning of the year. I knew other students were listening and I wanted to make sure Aria felt comfortable, so I tried to act excited, but also like it was no big deal.

Her face lit up, "Yes." She pulled out her phone and showed me a picture of her four-year-old daughter. My own daughter was only three years old at that time. Aria, who was 17 years old and a sophomore, had come to America two years prior from Sudan and had never mentioned her daughter to anyone at school. No one ever asked.

Missing pieces started to fall into place in my mind. The reasons why she was so tired in class everyday and why she didn't always finish the homework were now clear. She didn't have time between taking care of her daughter, her grandmother and working at the local grocery store to pay the bills. The stories that the students shared were so raw and insightful. I wanted them to be able to share their writing with their families and showcase not only their growth as a writer, but also their perspectives on their experiences.

During that first year, the students turned their three-page short stories into me and I was so blown away by how much I had learned. I asked some of the students if I could share their stories with our other teachers. They were surprised that other teachers would actually want to read their stories. Once I got permission, I shared the stories with my colleagues and they were equally surprised with what they learned. From what type of environment in which the student lived, to family tragedies, they were learning more about the students. This, in turn, helped teachers to develop better connections with the students and in the curriculum.

After that year, I knew that I had to find a way to share my students' stories on a large scale. I was so touched by the stories and how they helped to create empathy and understanding amongst my students. I got to know my students on a much deeper level than any of the other teachers. I wanted other teachers, students and the community to better understand the reasons as to why and how our refugee and immigrant neighbors leave their native lands. I knew that I needed to help share the voice of my students. In addition, the stories would help our teachers connect with these students and therefore facilitate better differentiation for those who needed it.

The next year, I decided to build upon the narrative writing unit and instead of students simply turning in a printed copy of their stories to me, I combined them and published them in a book. Students went through a similar writing process as the year before, but I included sample stories from the year before as examples and students also created a timeline of their lives. The timeline helped the students brainstorm the point in their lives that they wanted to write about.

Using my own money, I put together the students' stories and sent it to our district's print shop. They printed 50 copies of the book with a spiral binding and a plastic see-through cover.

Each student received two copies and then I gave the rest of the books to our administration, counselors, some teachers and local libraries. Students also uploaded their stories as a free ebook on the Flipsnacks website and I linked those to our class website. As people began to read the stories, they were excited to learn more about the background and culture of our EL students.

As teachers and administration shared the stories, the students were interviewed by local radio stations and news outlets. I even took two students to a school board meeting to share their stories. Our students also read their stories for some of the pre-service teachers at the university and our school staff of about 100 teachers.

"My two brothers, parents and I were hiding under the bed. We heard people screaming outside, men, women and children. I was scared and started to cry. My mom told me to be quiet so they wouldn't hear us," *Natasha said.

"I had no idea," one of the English teachers whispered to me with tears in her eyes.

Four of my students were presenting their stories to the staff during an all-school professional development session that I organized. I wanted to remind teachers that it is important to create relationships with EL students. Understanding their stories helps teachers become more empathetic and opens doors for communication. When teachers understand their students, they are better able to provide specialized instruction and accommodations for students.

After the story presentations, students sat together in the front of the room and took questions from the teachers. Hearing directly from the students about what they need, gives teachers a unique and essential perspective of how to better teach and understand students.

"What is the hardest part of school?" one teacher asked.

"That would probably be when some teachers talk too fast and I don't know what they are saying. My EL teachers don't do that but when I am in other classes, with American kids, that happens. I feel too embarrassed to raise my hand and ask questions," *Sandra answered. The other three students nodded.

"I would add that it is hard to do homework at home when EL students first come, because usually no one can help at home. My mom didn't know English, so she couldn't help me. Also, I have to watch my brothers and I work part time so I can help pay the bills. So, yeah, it would be nice not to have so much homework, or you could just stop giving homework to everyone," *Max said with a huge grin. His smile was infectious and that made most of the teachers in the room smile, knowing Max's humor.

After the session, I noticed the music teacher talking with one of the students, *Ranjir, and then he came over to me. He told me that he had just found out that Ranjir played the guitar in his refugee camp and had asked to join the school band. Unfortunately, our high school did not offer beginning band or instrument classes, because students started those in middle school. This was the reason why almost no EL students were able to learn how to play or continue to play an instrument in school. Because of what he learned from Ranjir, the band teacher offered up his lunch hours a couple days a week to give Ranjir guitar lessons.

Excited for the possibilities of giving students the ability to share their stories, I applied for the Eleanor Laing Law Literacy Grant in 2015 and received funding to implement a more integrative project that would help boost engagement, create empathy, not only amongst my students but also in the community, and empower my students to share their voices. I decided to use the stories as a vehicle to create a cohesive project that married multiple units together. The project spanned these units: "all about you," short story, grammar, technology, narrative writing, poetry and public speaking. These were already units within my curriculum before the project was started.

The units took place between September and January. I figured out a way to incorporate each unit within the project, so that the students could showcase their learning in a more tangible and empowering way. Tying together units in this way helped student engagement, since they had some prior knowledge about what they were learning.

For example, when students were working within the poetry unit, their final project was to create an I am From poem, which is based off of their stories that they previously created. Students had already brainstormed and written their experiences coming to the United States, so they were able to pull ideas from their story. In addition, grammar was not taught as a separate unit, it was incorporated throughout every unit. Grammar mini lessons and feedback within their stories helped students to grasp grammar concepts in a natural and meaningful way. During the speech unit, students learned the elements of public speaking by practicing with their stories.

For their final assessment, students presented their stories to a live audience at the local universities. After the project was completed, the remainder of the year consisted of units for a novel, career readiness and Romeo and Juliet. To accomplish the year's curriculum successfully, it is imperative that my students first understood and exhibited engagement and empathy.

Empathy is an important skill for all students to understand. I realized from early on that as an EL teacher, I needed to build deeper relationships and create a comfortable, trusting environment for my students. When teaching refugee and immigrant students with trauma, limited or interrupted education and possible undiagnosed learning disabilities, connection and trust are crucial. I needed to be intentional with teaching empathy and social emotional skills.

I started every year with an "All about you" unit. Taking time for students to get to know me and each other on a deeper level, was the key to effective learning and teaching. I incorporated opportunities that helped students understand and explore effective communication, mindfulness, their own personalities and their strengths and weaknesses. Students also took part in trust and team building activities such as relay races and leading each other blindfolded through the hallways. These activities were vital for my students to work and communicate effectively in my class.

Many students had a hard time trusting others and suffered emotional or physical trauma, so as result, would build up walls. Most of the time, this was evident by their shyness or lack of engagement, but sometimes it would surface through inappropriate attention seeking behaviors. *Albert was a great example of the latter.

Albert was a star athlete and had come to the United States when he was in ninth grade. Not only did Albert suffer from emotional trauma, but he also had an undiagnosed neurodivergence. Due to his outbursts in class, lack of completing work, and the fact that he had limited English abilities, it wasn't until he was a senior in high school that teachers were able to refer him to special services.

"Your hair is ugly," Albert yelled to a student across the room, as he was walking into class one day.

I had just complimented the student on his nice haircut when, not even seconds later, Albert came barreling into the room. Albert's deflective behavior became a problem, as he continued to spout obscenities at anyone who he thought was looking at him funny. Although sports came easy to Albert, academics did not, due to his neurodivergence. He could not focus and write his story, and often fell asleep in class due, in part, to his emotional trauma. Albert's behaviors were partly covering up the fact that he knew he struggled with reading and writing. Other students would catch on when he was not able to read out loud as fluently as them or when he would not know the answer when called on. So, Albert became the bully and class clown, drawing attention away from his academic work and to his behavior instead.

As we started to do more team building exercises as a class, there were moments that Albert was able to take the lead and, in those moments, Albert's inappropriate behaviors would disappear. I realized that Albert needed to feel a sense of control and success in the classroom, so I started to give him tasks to help me. I referred to him, jokingly at first, as my assistant teacher and after some resistance, he obliged. I had him help me with attendance, stand in front and go over worksheets (with my answer key) and help turn off the lights when we were doing mindfulness.

I started to see a change in Albert. As his confidence grew, his outbursts lessened and his attention improved. He started to participate in our daily mindfulness and team building activities. He started to trust me and his classmates and this allowed me to get to know him more. He was willing to share more about himself with me, engage in the lessons and often stayed after class to ask for help.

Most of the students understood exactly why I was asking Albert to help me with tasks in class, so when they would see him take charge, I would see the empathetic smiles on their faces. Not only did this experience help our students to engage with the content and empathize with each other on a deeper level, it also helped to empower Albert and make him comfortable with attempting to answer a question or do an assignment, even if he wasn't sure of the answers.

He had told me at the start of the year that he wasn't going to write his story or present it. So the day he came to my class with a paragraph of his story he had written at home on his own, I was surprised. It was already a week late, but I didn't mention that. I praised him for his efforts and he smiled and said, "Okay, I'm done now right?" He must have seen the confusion on my face, because he followed that up with, "Nah, just kidding Ms. J."

While writing his story, even though he got frustrated by not being able to use correct grammar to express himself, he kept on trying. Not every day was a good day for Albert, but I was so proud of his progress and his willingness, in the end, to complete and present his story.

In 2015, the grant also helped to bring Sudanese Lost Boy and CEO, John Dau, to our school to inspire the whole student body with his message of resilience and hope. After a school-wide assembly, he came into our classroom and worked with the students through a writing workshop. His story of fleeing war, walking thousands of miles and drinking his own urine to survive helped to inspire my students to believe in themselves and to not be ashamed of where they came from. I remember one of my students asking him, "do you ever feel alone, even when you are around people?"

John was honest and answered, "Yes, I have felt that my whole life." The student smiled a little and John went on to talk about his experiences as a refugee and an author. My heart sank listening to their conversations and hearing that my students felt alone. At the same time, the excitement that my students showed and their eagerness to start brainstorming their own stories, made my heart soar. You could sense the empathy that my students felt for John and vice versa. John talked about persistence and by the time he left, my students started to feel empowered to share their own stories.

In 2016, I applied for the grant again and ended up receiving funding for a total of six consecutive years. Each year, I improved or added more pieces to the project. I continued to start off our Journey to America project with an inspirational immigrant or refugee speaker. The first day of speakers was called our kick-off and the whole school was invited to the event.

Over the years, speakers at our event included Burundian refugee, author and CEO Laetitia Mizero Hellerud, as well as, Rwandan genocide survivor, LGBTQ (Lesbian, Gay, Bisexual Transgender, Queer) advocate and CEO, Daniel Trust. I remember when Daniel was onstage in our theater during his presentation. I had invited teachers to bring their classes to the event and the large theater was almost filled. There was a moment in Daniel's presentation where a student asked if he was married. "No, I am not. But if you know of any successful, good looking, single men, please let me know," he said with a grin. The whole theater erupted in applause. I was surprised by such a positive reaction from the students. Being a conservative midwestern city, I knew that many people had differing opinions on such topics. Daniel had not revealed his sexuality before that moment, so many were surprised by his candid answer.

Later, when I was walking Daniel out of the school, a tall girl dressed in a cheerleading uniform approached us. "Daniel! Can I get a selfie with you?" He smiled and told her he was happy to take a picture with her. After the photo, the girl continued, "Your story was amazing. I am also LGBTQ and I'm so happy to meet you!" As we continued to walk down the hall, he was stopped every couple feet for more selfies. The students' reactions were more than I hoped for and due to the positive experience, I sought out more role models to share their stories with my students.

I invited additional refugee and immigrant adults from our community to come to our classroom. Other speakers also inspired the students throughout the unit. During the 2020–2021 pandemic, speakers joined our class by Zoom. Along with former students, celebrity Kalen Allen from The Ellen Show talked with students about his journey to stardom and inspired them to share their stories and be true to themselves.

Having my students write and present narratives is a delicate process. The recognition that they receive helps students to process the events and move forward. The process can be therapeutic for some students. Some students are even ready and willing to write about traumatic events, and others are not. It is important that teachers do not try to make students write something they are not comfortable with. Oftentimes when refugees are forced to recount their experiences, to satisfy the curiosity of others, it can re-traumatize them. I make sure my students all understand that they have total control over what they write and present.

Considering the immense amount of trauma that many of my students had faced, it was beneficial to bring in experts to help facilitate some activities and to address underlying trauma. I found a local organization, Imagine Thriving, that came into my classroom and helped facilitate some difficult conversations. At first, I wasn't sure how my students would respond, considering mental health and emotions are often not addressed in their native cultures. During the first session, I was pleasantly surprised at how many students were eager to participate. Their questions were thoughtful, but also heartbreaking. "What does it mean if you cry yourself to sleep every night? Are you depressed?" one student asked. "I get sad, but I would never kill myself. I would just cut myself a little, but not much anymore. Other people do that too, right?" the student commented, as she held up her scarred wrists. I'll never forget how nonchalantly those words came out of the student's mouth. I was stunned and didn't know what to say. My heart sank and the other students sat silently. I don't even remember what the counselor said, but it was a great response that made everyone comfortable and reassured that we were in a safe space.

The students received information about resources to use when they needed to talk to someone or if they needed help addressing mental health issues. They were eager to take the information. I followed up with the school counselor and our EL social worker with the information that came out in our sessions and they were able to start working with certain students.

One of the biggest challenges to providing mental health services to EL students is the cost of the services. Counseling and therapy are expensive and many of my students do not have insurance coverage that pays for those services. In addition, it is very difficult for many families and students to get past the stigma that addressing mental health means that someone is weak or crazy. Addressing the issues related to trauma and mental health certainly helped pave the way for many students to know where to start writing their stories.

During the writing workshop stage of the project, university students, professors and community members volunteered with us for eight weeks. I was lucky to connect with university professor, Kevin Brooks, and he was eager to set up an after school tutoring program. I helped him arrange the program, but we found that students were not able to stay after school, due to transportation issues. We moved the program to tutoring during school hours, in the library or study halls.

At one point, that turned into having his English major students come into the classroom and help out with the writing workshop. Kevin helped spread the word about my need for volunteers, and eventually, I had over 100 students and professors from all three local universities, as well as community volunteers working with my students throughout the project. The EL students were responsible for the typing of the story on their laptops and the volunteers sat with them to help brainstorm more ideas or help with grammar questions. Students receive help with the technical writing of their stories, but also end up connecting with the volunteers on a more personal level.

"So, where do you work?" I heard a student ask her to volunteer, while they were working together.

"At Claires, in the mall. It is a pretty fun job," the university student replied.

"That sounds fun. I am looking for a job," my student answered.

"Do you want me to bring you an application? I can help you fill it out. We should be hiring soon," the university student said with a smile.

"Really? That would be good," my student said with a smile. Even though they were off-task, I didn't say anything. I was happy that my students were making connections within the community, something that so many of them lacked. My students gained confidence, as they talked with their partners. They also felt as if they were important, because their partner was paying attention to them. Volunteers learned a lot about the cultures of those students that they helped. For some, it was the first time they have worked with someone who doesn't look like them. This was in part, due to the fact that many college students who go to our local universities come from small rural, non-diverse communities from around North Dakota and Minnesota.

It was great to see the students start opening up and sharing more details about their hardships and their journeys as the volunteers encourage them throughout the process. Students always had the choice of how they wanted to tell their stories. Some chose to start their stories at the moment they found out they were coming to the United States, while others wanted to start their stories with important events. Some also simply started their stories from the day they landed in America and went to their new homes. It was important to me that students feel comfortable with whatever they ended up writing. Since the writing was shared with a large audience, the student should have felt like it was a true portrait of themselves. I made sure they knew that they would be publishing the stories and reading them to the public. I advised them to not share anything they didn't feel comfortable sharing.

Many of my students were older than average and between the ages of 17 and 21. When we started the project, I sent home information about the project and permission forms for guardians and students to sign to participate in the publishing of the stories. Throughout all of the years of the project, I have only had one guardian not consent to the project. That was understandable due to the fact that the student was an unaccompanied refugee minor and had to keep their story private at that time. Students had total control of their stories, so I was surprised at how many wanted to write about difficult, and often tragic experiences.

"As I was standing by someone, I heard a gunshot. I thought that they had shot me, but when I looked, I saw the person that was standing beside me was shot. She died immediately," I read quietly from a student's computer. She had called me over to check her story so far, since she had added a whole new paragraph. "*Emma, I'm so sorry. That must have been really hard."

"Yeah," Emma said, just shrugging her shoulders. Students were about one page into their four-page stories at that point and I wanted to make sure Emma knew that she was going to present whatever she wrote.

"You know, you don't have to write anything that you are not comfortable with sharing. You will be reading this out loud and having it published in a book and online. Make sure to write only what you want to share with other people," I said.

"Eh, it's what happened," Emma said with absolutely no expression on her face. She then turned and continued to type her story. I stood there for a moment in disbelief at her ambivalence to such a tragic event and her willingness to share it. I started to understand more and more just how strong, resilient and emotionally scarred my students were.

In addition to the story, students wrote an "About the Author" page about themselves and included a picture. A language glossary was also added to every story because the students included words and phrases from their native language within their stories. During this part of the project, I was surprised at how many students were not able to translate English back into their written native language. I found out that many were not literate in their first language.

During the third year of the project, students also added their I AM FROM poems from our poetry unit to the book. In addition, students visited the art museum, received a tour and painted a scene from their story on a large canvas, provided by the museum. These were then showcased at our public reading at the end of the project.

Once students finished the writing and editing process of their stories and their poems, they created an e-book and posted it on our class website (www.ELLfargosouth.weebly.com). Every year, students have created artwork for the cover of the hard copy book that we print. In 2020, I ordered over 600 copies and mailed them to a teacher in every state, one of the perks of being a state teacher of the year. I also mail them to education organizations, libraries, universities, other schools and throughout the local community.

"Bang, bang, bang! I suddenly heard gunshots! *'Mushitoke mu fuge melango!'* my neighbor shouted. People were crying, screaming, and running," junior, *Naima, started reading in a somber voice. Minutes later, as she was nearing the end of her three-minute excerpt that she chose to read for our public reading at the local university, I heard her voice start to waver. She read, "My grandfather knew he wasn't going to make it. We were only about half a mile away from the refugee camp when he died. We couldn't carry him, so we had to leave his body in the forest..." At that moment her eyes filled with tears and she turned away from the microphone. During our two weeks of practice, Naima had practiced countless times and read through her story without tears or much emotion. On this day, reading out loud for an audience made everything seem so real and her emotions came flooding back.

I rushed up to the front and comforted her with a hug. I asked her if she wanted to continue, as students have done the same in the past. She shook her head and I told her she could just say "to be continued." I sent another student with her, as she made her way out of the room. I quickly introduced the next student and then snuck out to talk to Naima. She was in the hallway, bent over, wiping tears from her face. "I'm so sorry. I don't know why I started crying. I didn't before. I'm sorry I ruined the reading," she sobbed.

"What? No way, you didn't ruin anything. Tears don't mean you are weak, they mean you are real. You are such a strong, resilient young woman. Never apologize for that. You are honoring the memory of your uncle and grandfather and they would be so proud of you!" I said with tears in my eyes. She nodded, smiled, and then asked if she could go back and finish reading her story. The resilience that my students exhibited astounded me.

This was the culminating activity for the project. Students participated in a public reading at two different local universities. The students practiced their stories or poems, using techniques that they learned in the previous speech unit. University students also came and practiced with the students. Students read a three to a four-minute excerpt of their story or their whole poem in front of a public audience. I coordinated the event initially with my former university advisor. She reserved the room and took care of the logistics. Many university students and professors would attend the presentations. My students were especially excited to see the university students, who had volunteered with them in the classroom.

In addition to the stories and poems, my students wanted to also showcase their other talents. Over the years, between readings, we have had students sing, dance and play instruments. In addition to this, the students had their artwork displayed on the stage, so that people could admire their hard work.

For two years, I invited the other high school in our area, that also had the same level of EL students, to join our project. They wrote their stories and also presented with us at the university. In 2019, my friend Mandy Manning, Washington state EL teacher and the 2018 National Teacher of the Year, joined our presentation at the university and gave the opening speech. My students were honored that she was there for their presentation. The students dressed up in clothing from their native cultures or their best formal wear for the presentation.

The feeling I get after watching one of my students confidently read their story to a public audience, in their second, third or even fourth language, is indescribable. I beam with pride, often holding back tears as I watch them in amazement.

Since our first public reading of the Journey to America Stories, my students have won awards from the Scholastic Art and Writing Contest, as well as the Reflections Contest. My students and their stories have been featured in magazines, internet blogs, podcasts, literary journals, newspapers, the news and on the radio. They have shared their stories at nursing homes, schools, local conferences, professional development conferences for teachers and even partnered with a local theater company to spread cultural awareness. Through this project, they have been empowered to make a difference.

Teachers often wonder if what they have done ever makes a difference in their students' lives. Teachers give so much of themselves to their students and oftentimes are left wondering if it was ever enough. Many teachers never get the satisfaction of seeing a student grow and mature over the years. Since I am the only EL English teacher for our student body, I have the privilege of watching my students blossom and become proficient in their English and their academic skills. One of the most gratifying moments in my teaching career happened during the summer of 2017.

"Ms. J! Can you come to my church next week?" Aline asked on the other end of the phone.

"What's going on?" I asked curiously.

"My sister and I are having a ceremony for our family and we want you to come," she said excitedly. It was the beginning of August when I received an unexpected phone call from Aline. I had just given birth to my son in April, so my summer had been pretty relaxed and I was happy to hear from Aline. I had always attended my students' activities in school and outside of school when I could, so it was not a big surprise to get this invitation.

"Sure, when is it?" I asked, still not exactly understanding what I was going to do. I got all of the details, and when the day came, my four-month-old son and I headed over to the church. When I walked in, I was greeted with smiles. The lobby and church were filled with Aline's friends and family, some of whom drove across the country just to be there. I wasn't sure where to go and walked around, looking for a familiar face. Nothing looked like it had started yet, so I wasn't sure where to go.

"Ms. J!" I heard a familiar voice yell. I turned around and saw two of my EL students, who also came from Burundi and Congo. "I'm so glad you are here! Oh, look at him, he is so cute!" one student said, referring to my son. I asked her if she knew where Aline was and where I should go. She led me to the main sanctuary of the church, where some people had started to gather. I sat down and soon Aline and her sister came up to me and gave me big hugs.

"I am so glad you are here. We will start soon," Aline said. I nodded and just as I was about to say something, someone called her attention and she was rushed away. It seemed like she was busy coordinating everything.

About 20 minutes later, Aline came back and sat by me, just as a man started talking loudly in Kirundi into an echoing microphone. "Do you want me to translate for you?" Aline asked me with a smile. I could tell that her family standing nearby wanted her to follow them up front.

"No, that is okay, you go, I'll be fine," I said.

"Ok, Ms. J. It will be like school in Kirundi for you. I will give you a test afterwards, so pay attention," she replied as she walked up front to sit with her family.

I sat and listened to the beautiful songs, and the passionate speakers. At one point a group of women got up to speak and even though I did not know what they were talking about, I had a feeling that because of their tears and their sadness that they were talking about Aline's father.

The ceremony continued for about an hour. Then everyone was ushered into the reception area, where there was a buffet of delicious African food. My students certainly know how much I love trying new food. I got a plate and sat at an empty table. Eventually, the only other White woman in the church came over to sit by me. She was a social worker and introduced herself.

After getting food, Aline and her sister came over and sat next to me as I was giving my baby a bottle. "So what did you think?" Aline asked.

"It was a beautiful ceremony and this food is amazing," I said with a smile. "So was this a family ceremony?"

Aline looked at me curiously and said, "Well, yeah, but it was for my dad mainly. My sister and I organized all of it. We have family and friends that drove here from many different states."

"Wow, that is really neat. So this is a memorial for your dad? It's been about 8 years since he passed away, haven't you had a memorial yet?" I asked.

"No, Ms. J. We never talked about my dad in our house after he died. It was too hard," Aline said.

"Oh, so why now?" I asked.

"Because of you, Ms. J. Because of your class and the stories. When my sister and I started writing our stories, that was the first time we had ever talked about our dad since he passed away. It was so hard, but each time I read the story, it got easier and I started to feel better, like a weight was lifted off my shoulders," Aline replied, as she motioned to her shoulder.

*I was speechless. Tears welled up in my eyes and I fought to hold them back. As a teacher, it was hard to put into words how much that meant to me. If there were ever days that I felt discouraged, I reminded myself of how lucky I was to be in a position where I could make a difference in a student's life, whether I knew it or not.*

## Concluding Thoughts

I work hard to create a welcoming environment for my EL students to thrive in. Integrating the Journey to America project into my curriculum was not an easy task, but I knew it was something that would benefit my students in so many ways. It is important to encourage students to engage with each other and the curriculum, as well to create a classroom that fosters empathy and understanding. If you are able to do that, then you and your students will feel empowered to learn new things and advocate, using voices for things that matter the most to you.

##  Reflection Questions

1. What do you do to create empathy in your classroom?
2. What do you do to engage students in your classroom?
3. What do you do to empower your students?
4. How might you involve the community in your classroom?
5. Are there units that you could combine, using a common theme?
6. What was the most gratifying moment of your career as an educator?
7. Do you empower students to advocate for what they believe in?

*Names in this chapter have been changed.

# 6

# Sharing Stories and Creating Partnerships

## Green Card Youth Voices: Immigration Stories From a Fargo High School

"I hate this class. It isn't even a class," Muhend yelled, as he headed for the door again.

"When you decide to come back, I'll be here to help you with your homework. Just let me know," I said with a smile.

"I'm not coming back," I heard the sophomore yell, and then he started to laugh, just as the door slammed shut.

I headed over to my computer and sent a quick email to the office to let them know the student had left, again, during resource class. EL students were assigned a resource class with an EL teacher instead of a study hall once they started taking more than one mainstream core class or if they had exited the EL program.

Muhend Abakar came to the United States in 2012 and started 8th grade with an ELL ACCESS level 1 English proficiency, and by sophomore year of high school, he was a level 4. This was a faster than normal progression in levels than most of our students make. Usually students take four or more years to reach level 4. Muhend had a decent educational background in Egypt, where he had lived most of his life. When he was four

DOI: 10.4324/9781003177333-9

years old, his life was upset by the war in South Sudan, and that forced his family to move to Egypt.

Muhend's parents had high expectations for him and his younger siblings and were supportive when I would have to make the call home about their son skipping class. Muhend was also in my English 4 class and was going through his Journey to America story project that same year. He was also taking some mainstream classes. It is quite a jump to go from an EL core class to a mainstream class for some students, due to past interrupted or limited access to education. The next year, he was to go to a mainstream English class.

Our EL students enrolled in mainstream 9th grade English, no matter what grade they were in after completing EL English 4. If students were seniors, then they were able to graduate, since the EL English credits count toward graduation. So, to give students extra support, they were enrolled in a resource class, which had fewer students and an EL teacher, who they are familiar with, to provide help with homework. Even though study and grammar skills were often taught as bell ringers, students do not earn credit from the class, since the main prerogative was for them to work on their homework.

Muhend was a lean, tall natural athlete, and made many friends through sports. He had a magnetic personality and would talk to anyone. Muhend hated having an assigned resource. He said it felt like a jail to him. He was a social butterfly and did not understand why, as a sophomore, he had to have a resource class, rather than an open campus free period to hang out with his friends. Generally, only freshmen were assigned to a study hall, but our EL students, of all grades, were assigned to a resource, if they fit the criteria. This was a key intervention for the EL students, since the majority of them did not have anyone at home that spoke English and therefore did not have anyone to help them with homework.

Muhend's loquacious nature often caused him to be late, or would get him in trouble during class. Luckily, for him, he had a great sense of humor. When a teacher would question his behavior, he often met them with a humorous remark and a big smile. It was hard not to like Muhend.

"I'm back!" Muhend yelled as he walked in, disrupting the quiet classroom minutes before the bell was about to ring. He was carrying an open carton of milk and a bag of Hot Takis.

"You know the rules, no food in class, you need to put those away or throw them away," I said, shaking my head.

"So you are making me leave? Ok, see ya!" he said, walking out the door with a big smile.

Toward the end of the year, I saw some little changes in Muhend. After reading his Journey to America story at the university for his EL English 4 class, he left class less and less. He became more focused. He had loved presenting his story in front of an audience and he began to feel empowered. He seemed to trust me and understood that resource class was not a punishment, but a way to help. He started to come (mostly) on time and stay in the room during class. I can't say he was always productive, but he did make an effort. It wasn't until two years later that I got to see Muhend really come into his own, as an author in our book Green Card Youth Voices: Immigration Stories from a Fargo High School.

Being able to watch students mature, overcome challenges and find their passions is one of the best things about being able to teach some of the same students year after year. I love encouraging students to step outside their comfort zones and try new things. Knowing how amazing my students are and how much they have to contribute to society, I jumped at the chance to have them share their stories further, with the organization, Green Card Voices (GCV).

At the beginning of the 2016–2017 school year, the success of the Journey to America project connected me with the director of GCV, a Minneapolis, Minnesota based organization that shared the stories of immigrants and refugees from around the nation.

Started by Tea Rozman-Clark, GCV is a non-profit that was founded in 2015 and aimed to connect refugees and immigrants with their communities through storytelling in various ways. Rozman-Clark, an immigrant from Slovenia, received a prestigious Bush Fellowship to fund her initiative. The organization first created "Voices of Immigrant Storytellers: Teaching Guide for Middle and High Schools," followed by their first book of high school refugee and immigrant authors, Green Card Youth Voices: Immigration Stories from a Minneapolis High School (https://www.greencardvoices.org). In addition to the book, students are recorded telling their story and the videos are made accessible on the website.

It was the spring of 2016 when I opened up my email to a message from Kevin Brooks, the university professor who had been sending his student to volunteer in my class for the Journey to America project. "Hey Leah, check out what this organization is doing, it reminded me of your project!" I clicked on the link and read about the GCV initiative. Brooks and Rozman-Clark had crossed paths recently, since they were both Bush Fellows. As I read more about GCV, thoughts started to race in my head. Their initiative was to record stories of refugee and immigrant students for every state. One of the things that I loved about the organization was that all of the adults working with the project were also refugees or immigrants.

From that moment, I knew I just had to partner with them. This was an amazing opportunity for my students to share their stories with a larger audience. GCV had a professional videographer, photographer and grant money to carry out the project and to produce books that could be sold on Amazon. So, within minutes of receiving the initial email, connecting me with Rozman-Clark, I was crafting an email to GCV explaining who I was, how I heard about them and detailing our Journey to America project. I explained that I would love to have my students work with them. I had no idea if I would ever get a response, but it was worth a try. Needless to say, I got a response soon after, and Rozman-Clark and I planned to start the six-month project in the fall of 2016.

When school started in the fall, Rozman-Clark and I met with my principal to outline the project and get the necessary permission. We decided to open up the project to current and exited EL high school students of any level. I spread the word to all of my students and even headed to the cafeteria during lunch to find former students to tell about the opportunity. I created a sign up sheet and taped it to my board.

It wasn't difficult to get students to participate. In fact, I had too many students who wanted to take part in the project and

I ended up having to turn some away. I think students were interested, because they knew about the success of the Journey to America project and trusted me enough to know that I was presenting them with a good opportunity.

So, how did I choose which students participated in the GCV project? The students had varying English language skills. One requirement was that they needed to be able to express themselves orally in English enough so that they could answer questions during the recorded interview. Another consideration was that since we had a large variety of students from many different countries, the first thing I looked for was a variety of countries, based on whoever signed up first.

Low and behold, one of the first was Muhend. The student who told me he hated resource class and was found walking the halls instead of being in my English 4 class just two years earlier. Now, as a senior, track star, varsity soccer player and a photographer for the school newspaper, everyone knew Muhend. He had matured and had been accepted to the local four year university.

In the end, 31 students from 21 different countries were selected for the project.

1. Sudan
2. Chad
3. Nepal
4. Democratic Republic of the Congo
5. Eritrea
6. Burma
7. China
8. Sierra Leone
9. Nigeria
10. Zambia
11. Iraq
12. Côte d'Ivoire
13. Liberia
14. Togo
15. Tanzania
16. Mexico

17. Kenya
18. Vietnam
19. Somalia
20. Ethiopia
21. Egypt

After identifying the participating students, I had a meeting to explain the project and the permission forms, if they were under 18 years old. Since they were going to be participating in a project that produced an online video and a book, it was necessary for them to give their permission, as well as to get permission from a parent or guardian. I met with the students multiple times before and after school and during off periods to give them some advice about presenting and to talk with them about the interview questions.

GCV asked the same six questions to every student during the interview.

1. Tell us about what you remember about your country.
2. Why did you move?
3. Describe the journey.
4. How was it when you first got to the US/Fargo?
5. How is your life now?
6. What are your hopes and dreams?

During the first phase of the project, the GCV crew came to our school and set up a recording studio in one of the theater dressing rooms. I created a spreadsheet with each student's name, native country and blocks of time that they would go to the recording studio to film their interview. I tried my best to make sure students were interviewed during their off hours or study halls, as not to interrupt their classes. Over a one-week period, students were individually interviewed and recorded in the studio. Students then signed up for a time to get their pictures taken by the photographer. Some students even traveled downtown, using local landmarks as backgrounds for their pictures.

"Ms. J, I can't do my interview or take my picture today!" senior student, Divine Lubungo exclaimed.

Because our program feels like a family, many of my students misguidedly think it is okay just to walk in the room while I am in the middle of teaching. This was the case with Divine. She walked right in, while I was in the middle of teaching a class. I calmly told her to wait in the hall and I would be right out. I was coordinating the GCV project on top of teaching a full schedule of classes. When I stepped into the hall, Divine was standing there, looking upset.

"I forgot my picture was today and I haven't finished braiding my hair. I can't go today," she puffed. Divine was one of my "originals," just like Muhend. She was a part of the very first year of the Journey to America project. After that year, Divine continued in my resource class, since she was still classified as EL, but took on more mainstream classes.

Divine was a self-proclaimed tomboy, whose favorite pastime was climbing mango trees in her native country of Congo. But you couldn't tell that by looking at her. Being that both of these students had huge personalities, there were definitely times that Muhend and Divine butted heads. Like the time when Divine and Muhend argued about the difficulty level of the social studies homework. When he wouldn't agree with her, she refused to do any work for the whole hour because she was too angry. Then there was the time when Muhend told Divine that she talked too much. That resulted in Divine giving the silent treatment to myself and everyone in the class for two days. Oh, and of course, there was the time when Muhend left to go to the bathroom, but came back with a bag of chips. Before I could even say anything, Divine sarcastically reminded him of the no food rule and tried to take the bag away from him. This resulted in another argument and in the end, I had a bag of chips for lunch.

I know teachers aren't supposed to have favorites, but these two kids were definitely two of my favorites. They were both spunky, smart, had a great sense of humor and were natural born leaders. They were also very different. Muhend had come to the U.S. from Egypt with his parents, siblings and a solid educational background. Divine lived in war-torn Congo with her older sister, who became her guardian and her brothers. Divine's education was interrupted due to the war and she found herself in Uganda before being resettled in the U.S. without her parents. Despite the challenges these two faced as refugees, they were both still persistent and hopeful. Their resilience continues to inspire me to this day.

"Your hair looks fine," I reassured her in a motherly tone. But she wasn't having it.

"Really? Really? You think I am going to put my picture in the book with hair looking like this? Sure, why not?" she yelled in a sarcastic tone. She gave me a look that told me that she was not going to change her mind. I smiled. After knowing Divine for three years, I understood how persistent she was. I ended up letting her reschedule her interview and photo. I knew that this was important to her and to do her best, she needed to feel her best.

It was interesting to see students come back from their interviews and photo sessions. When I asked how it was, some students just shrugged and said fine. Other students told me that they were so bad and it was their worst interview ever, while others literally asked me if I wanted their autographs.

After the interviews and photos were wrapped up, the GCV crew left and then went to work on transcribing the interviews. Within a couple of weeks, they sent over the transcriptions to me and for a month, I sat down with each student and went through their transcriptions with them. We took out filler words like "um" and "uh," as well as things that the students said wrong or wanted to change. During this editing process, students were made aware of their spoken language errors. Many of them were in disbelief about the number of times they used filler words. This helped them become more conscious of those words when they spoke. This process lent to the creation of each of the students' written stories in the book. This process was different from my Journey to America project, because a student did not need to be able to write well to share their story. They only needed to be able to orally communicate their ideas. This allowed for students of lower levels to also participate. A modified version of this activity could easily be done in any classroom. Students could interview each other and then listen to their own interviews, pausing to write down every word they hear. Next, students would then work with a partner or teacher to revise and edit what they wrote down. The length of the interview would depend on the English level of the student.

Once the transcribing was completed, GCV visited our school again with the rough draft of the book. The students were in disbelief that the book was actually almost ready. As they looked over their drafts, the question I heard the most was "Can I retake my picture?" All of the pictures looked great, but when you work with teenagers, you know to expect this type of self-consciousness. After the proofing of the draft, it was time to get ready for the book launch party.

The book launch was a huge success. It was held in a local hotel conference room and was decorated with huge 10 ft tall banners with a picture of each student author on their own banner. Many members of the community attended, including our school district's superintendent, staff, teachers, social workers, police officers and families. North Dakota Senator, Heidi Heitkamp, even sent us a video message of congratulations that was played during the ceremony.

Students volunteered to showcase their talents, singing and dancing to start off the night. For the presentation, students prepared a short paragraph from their stories that they were to read out loud in front of the audience. It was humorous at times, as students either forgot their notes or went off and just started saying thank you to everyone like it was the Academy Awards.

When Muhend went up front to read his one-minute part, in true "Muhend fashion," he ditched his notes and went completely off script. He said, "Ah, I don't need this," and then literally crumpled up his notes and just started to tell a story. Since time was limited, everyone was supposed to stick to their short parts. Eventually, I had to catch his attention from the back of the room, give him the "teacher eye," and motion for him to wrap it up.

One of my favorite memories was when all of the students sat behind long tables at the end of the night, giving autographs to everyone who bought their books. When everyone was about to leave, one police officer had asked for an autograph and the tables had already been taken down. She ended up telling the student to use her back as a surface. I still have the image of the student smiling as she autographed the book, while using a police officer's back.

In March of 2018, I traveled with my GCV student authors to the first annual GCV Youth Leadership Summit in Minneapolis, Minnesota. The event brought student authors from the Minneapolis, St. Paul and the Fargo books together and was sponsored by the Minnesota Twins and the Malala Fund. My female students were interviewed by a representative from the Malala Fund and were featured on their website that summer.

During the summit, students visited the science museum and the baseball stadium. Students took part in sessions on public speaking, storytelling and writing. They also heard from a collection of diverse authors, politicians and CEOs, who inspired them to take leadership roles and to never give up. After that year, Muhend and Divine started to pursue more public speaking engagements and even got paid opportunities to share their stories with GCV. I asked both students to present with me at schools, conferences and on the radio during those years. During that time, Muhend continued to share his story around the state and even became an ambassador for GCV.

In 2019, I was presenting a session on Using Stories to Create Empathy at a statewide immigration conference with two of my current students. I had just finished the session and while I was walking down the hall, I saw Muhend! For a second, I thought that I had invited him and somehow forgot about it. That wasn't the case at all. Muhend was running a session on his own, representing GCV and their new Story Stitch project.

I attended his session in disbelief about how grown up he now was. I was so proud of him. He used to have an issue with rambling on and on. I remember during a radio interview that we did together, he completely took over and we couldn't get him to wrap up his story. He always had so much to say. I used to tell him: "clear and concise, you need to be clear and concise." As I watched this young man, who used to skip class and bring Hot Takis into my classroom, so effortlessly and expertly facilitate a session full of teachers, social workers and community members, I couldn't help but beam with pride.

As I walked out of his session, I couldn't believe my eyes. There was Divine. She was walking into one of the sessions. I called out her name and she let out a squeal. She ran over to me and gave me a big hug. She told me that she was there to present on a panel about unaccompanied minors and foster care. She didn't even know Muhend was there until I told her.

I couldn't believe how grown up Divine and Muhend were. It felt like yesterday that they were arguing about chips in my classroom. Now, here they were, presenting to large audiences, on their own!

Muhend went on to university and graduated with a double major in finance and accounting with a minor in math within just three years. Muhend moved to Washington state and plans to pursue motivational speaking and to attend graduate school to become a coach or administrator someday. The last time I saw him, he told me, "If you didn't push me like you did Ms. J, I would never be where I am today."

Divine served on the ND Foster Care Youth Board and worked at a bank while finishing college. She even came with me when I spoke at a local Women's March Rally. She stays in touch and continues to update me on her life.

High school students enrolled in World Culture classes at my school and college students around the nation are using our book as curriculum in their classes. This has also helped to spawn new partnerships. Those students who take the course using the book at Concordia College in Moorhead, MN volunteer in our class to also help with our Journey to America Project.

During the summer of 2020, I asked Muhend and Divine to help me virtually present about storytelling and GCV at the National Teacher's of the Year Conference. It was so much fun presenting with them one last time. It reminded me how lucky I am to be able to see my influence as a teacher. The experience assured me that all the extra work and long hours I put into the storytelling projects is definitely worth it. The connections and skills that these projects build are some of the most important keys to success for my students.

Providing these kinds of opportunities for my students to connect to the community is so important. As first-generation immigrants and refugees, my students and their families often struggle to establish themselves within society. I have learned that I am the one that has to reach out to the community if I want my student to have these experiences. Helping students connect and engage with the community could be as easy as inviting a speaker into the classroom, in person or virtually, that they can relate to or asking a nursing home or daycare if your students can visit and participate in their activities or read to them. You could partner with a local university and have students come to your class once a month. I have found that university students usually need volunteer hours, most likely drive and have availability during the day. Your students could draw a picture of an event they remember from their childhood and share it with their university buddy. You could even do five-minute rotations, and have students share with multiple buddies. One of the first steps to providing opportunities for your students like I have, is reaching out to the community and letting them know you want to connect. The projects that I have done continued to flourish due to my networking efforts. Yes, it was a lot of extra time and energy, but you don't have to come up with elaborate projects like mine to help your students connect with others. Providing opportunities, no matter how big or small, for your students to teach others or share about themselves creates empathy, engagement and empowerment.

## Partnership for New Americans

"Run! Come on, keep going!" I yelled to the students as they ran back and forth between cones on the front lawn of the school.

"Ms. J, can I use my hands? It keeps falling out!" a blonde haired, blue-eyed student pleaded, as she picked up the piece of cotton from the ground and put it back onto her spoon.

"No hands, just go a little slower if you need to," I said with a smile. The two girls, who had just met minutes before, started to giggle as they dropped the spoon and the cotton for the third time.

On the first day of school, I take all of my classes outside. I don't hand out a syllabus. I don't make them sit through a long lecture about the rules. I don't even tell them what we are going to do until I have led them out the door and onto the front lawn of the school. There, I introduce myself, partner them with another student and hand them a plastic spoon, cotton, scraps of fabric, a ball, instructions and other objects to use in the relay race. Students introduce themselves to each other and then I explain the rules and demonstrate how to do each part of the relay. I am careful not to partner up males and females, as there are some cultures that are not comfortable with physical contact between genders. My favorite class to do this activity with on the first day is my Partnership for New Americans (PNA) class. The giggles, awkward glances and smiles on the students' faces are priceless when they figure out what we are doing. Even though they don't speak the same native language as their partner, they always find a way to communicate, whether it is through body language, facial expressions or short phrases. Teamwork, effort and communication are what the PNA class is all about.

"YES! We are done! We are done! Did we win the relay?" Two boys ran up to me, huge smiles on their faces. *Kyle, a blonde, light skinned boy stood in front of me with his partner, Yusef, a dark skinned boy with curly short black hair. Out of breath and with sweat dripping down his face, Yusef smiled.

"Win?" he asked. Sixteen-year-old *Yusef had just arrived in the U.S. two weeks before school had started. He had come by himself from Eritrea. Students who end up arriving alone in the U.S. and are between the ages of 0–21 are considered unaccompanied refugee minors. They are placed in a foster family and assigned a case manager through Lutheran Social Services.

"You know, he's pretty fast!" Kyle told me.

"Yes, I saw, you guys did great. Did you tell him that you think he's fast?" I asked Kyle.

"I don't think he understands me," Kyle said awkwardly.

"Yusef, I see you have a translator on your phone? Can I see it?" I motioned for the phone in his back pocket. He looked a little confused. "Tigrinya?" I asked.

"Ah!" Yusef's eyes lit up. I had said the name of his native language, so he knew I wanted to translate something. He opened the app and handed me the phone. After I showed Kyle how to use it, they sat in the shade and used the app to communicate, while everyone else finished the relay.

The PNA Class, in which non-EL or exited EL students mentor new EL students, encourages cultural exchange, cultivates curiosity and promotes global citizenship. The class was piloted for two years during 2014 and 2015, at one of the high schools in our district. In 2016, I taught the first class of PNA at my school. The class offers mentorship opportunities to native English speakers and exited EL students, students who have achieved a passing score on the ACCESS test and are no longer considered EL students. EL students who have recently arrived in the United States, are the mentees and receive an elective credit for the class. Native English-speaking students or students who have exited out of the EL program, sign up to take the class for an elective credit and are considered the mentors. Including students who have exited the EL program adds another dimension to the partnerships. These students know what it is like to be an EL student and can teach from experience.

Students are paired up and tasked with completing projects and activities together. The class is one semester for mentors and a full year for mentees, meaning that a new group of mentees take over at the end of the semester. I often have mentors ask to stay a second semester though, since they end up enjoying the class. An alternate structure of this class is done at the neighboring high school. Instead of PNA, they call it Social Inclusion. Special needs students are paired up with a group of mentors for a quarter and at the same time, another group of mentors are paired up with EL students. At the end of the quarter, these groups switch. This is a great opportunity for all involved, but it does take a lot of collaboration between the groups to organize. Whatever the structure of the class, it is important that the teacher takes time to create a safe and comfortable environment for the students.

I always start the year by explaining to my students that the two most important things to bring to class are respect and a positive attitude. This helps set a safe and comfortable foundation for our class. Since the majority of their grades are how they interact with each other, it is especially important to create a welcoming environment for all students. I talk with my students about what vulnerability means and why it is important. We also talk about trust. Many of my EL students have a difficult time trusting others, due to unreliable people, negative experiences or trauma in their past. Being consistent with routines and enforcing classroom norms helps students feel more comfortable, as they know what to expect. Routine also helps students practice skills and behaviors that are expected of them. It is also important that I be consistent with my mood and energy as their teacher. Since many of my students have dealt with unreliable people in their lives, they need to see me as stable and reliable.

I continue to talk about respect and a positive attitude throughout the year. If there are ever any conflicts or issues, I circle back to the idea of a positive attitude and respect, so everyone is reminded that their actions do affect others. I also give praise to students, when I see them demonstrating these values in difficult situations. As a result, I have had very minimal behavior issues within my classroom. When behaviors are not an issue, students have a positive attitude and respect each other, students are more comfortable and open to learning.

The class covers many topics that help mentees to understand their new school and community, all while practicing their speaking, reading, listening and writing skills. Mentors learn communication skills and about new cultures and traditions. I always start class with a bell ringer that requires the partners to ask each other a question or explain something about themselves. For this class, there is no textbook, but mentees are given new folders and binders at the beginning of the year. The binder and folders are used as an organizational tool for their school work.

## Organization Day

Every Monday, mentees are given a homework planner for the week, along with an activity planner. Mentors help mentees look up their homework from the online platform and record it on their homework planner. If the teacher posts additional work in class, the students are expected to take out their binders and record the homework. Next, students plan out their week on the activity planner. With the help of their mentor, students project when they will be doing homework, working or doing after school activities. Mentors also help mentees record their current grades in their binders and teach them that worksheets from each class belong in their own folders within the binder. Mentees need to make sure the planners are filled in for the week, because every Friday, mentors check their binders with a rubric, to make sure they are tidy and up to date.

In the beginning of the year, mentors are given separate instruction as to what it means to be a mentor and strategies for communication. This is usually done in the hall, while the EL students are working on their organization or their homework. I also give each mentor a copy of a Journey to America book, so that they can read about the experiences of EL students within their school.

## Social Game Day

On Fridays, mentors grade their mentees binders with a rubric, while sitting away from the student. I do this so that the mentors do not feel peer pressured into marking a certain grade on the rubric. Students that need help or want to make sure they are on the right track, come to me and I help them if needed. When the binders are corrected and rubrics are turned in, the mentors sit with their mentee and talk about what they saw in the binders. The most anticipated part of class on Fridays is social game time. I start the year with get to know you games, which I have printed on huge poster boards and laminated. Each partner group gets one game board. The games look a lot like Candy Land, but instead of candy, each space has a question for the student who lands on it. I hand out dice and game pieces or actual pieces of candy that they can use as the game piece, and eat after they finish. The game titles include; All About You, Favorites and Name Three Things. Later in the year, students are free to choose games like Scrabble, Uno, Boggle, Pictionary or Life from my cupboard. I also let students play games in groups of four sometimes, as long as their partners are in their group. It is amazing to watch their interactions as the year progresses. I see how students learn patience, social skills and empathy all while playing games with a peer who looks different from them on the outside but feels the same as them on the inside. It is heartwarming to watch mentors and mentees teach each other new games as well. Generally, there is usually laughter in my classroom, but on Fridays, it definitely fills the room. Board games, cards and teacher created games are learning tools and can be used in any classroom to create empathy, engagement and empowerment.

## Places and Faces

It is important for students to know who is who and where important places are in the school. One of the first units we do in PNA is called Places and Faces. Students get a list of important staff members and places around the school. The mentor's job is to take the mentee to those people and places. When they meet a staff member, they must introduce themselves by saying their name, grade, when they came to the U.S. and where they are from. The mentee must speak in complete sentences. The staff member signs the form to signal that they talked to the student. Staff members on the list include, principals, librarians, custodians, nutrition services, counselors, secretaries, tech support and proctors. Students take three days to go around the school to find the places on the list and meet the people. I also email the staff members to let them know that the students are doing this unit and will be visiting them. They love meeting the students each year. For the Places and Faces test, I give mentees and mentors a powerpoint with the picture of each staff member and their name, along with a picture of each important place. They take time in class to study this and also to go on additional practice walks to find the places. To review, we play faces and places bingo. On the day of the test, all students have to match the face of the staff on the screen with the name on their test paper. Then, each mentor takes his/her mentee out of the classroom and tells them a location from the list. The mentee has to lead the mentor to the correct location. The mentor can't talk when being led and the mentee has to do this for all ten locations.

This is a great unit to do with any demographic of students, in any age. You would be surprised at how many non-EL students did not know all of the administrators or where everything was located in the school.

## Food Day

It is amazing how food can bring people together. This is why food day is one of my favorite days. Students bring their favorite food that has some connection to their family. Students can make the food themselves, or someone in their family can make it. Students take turns explaining how the food is significant to them and what is in the food. I noticed that non-EL students often brought sweet foods like cookies, jello or bars while the EL students often brought savory foods like soups, samosas, injera, rice and fish. Once everyone presented, then students were allowed to go through the food line and take a sample of whichever foods they wanted. There were usually no leftovers, but if there was, the students waiting outside my class often got first dibs. The great thing about food day is that no language skills are needed to enjoy food together. Once students try each other's food, they share a common bond. Weeks later, I have heard students joking around about being hungry and wanting more of a certain food they had tried. Food day would be a great activity for any class. There are many ways to connect food to the curriculum.

## Peer Teaching

Since mentors take on the role of a teacher within the class, I created a peer teaching unit. Each mentor chooses something that they are passionate about and teaches the class for the entire period. Mentors have to create a lesson plan on the template I give them and choose a day within the unit to teach their lesson. Some of the peer teaching lessons are:

1. Photography: the student brought in her tripod and expensive camera. She explained the basic elements of photography with a powerpoint. She then took a portrait of each student and later, printed them and gave them to the students.
2. Sewing: the student brought in fabric and showed the students how to sew a basic stitch. The students cut the fabric and made rectangular cell phone pockets.
3. Theater Games: the student brought the class to the school theater and played different theater games.

4. Yoga: the student brought the class to the dance/yoga studio in the school and had the students participate in yoga.

5. Brazilian Jiu Jitsu: the student brought the class to the school wrestling room, and taught some BJJ techniques.

6. Refugee Camps: the student shared a powerpoint about how she was raised in a Nepali refugee camp.

7. Soccer: the student brought the class to the school gym and taught soccer skills and played a game.

8. Vietnam/chopsticks: the student showed a powerpoint about Vietnamese New Year and food. She passed out chopsticks and grains of rice and had students see if they could pick up the rice with the chopsticks.

9. Nepali Dance: the student brought the class to the dance studio and showcased her Nepali dances. She then taught all students a dance.

10. Volleyball: the student brought the class to the school gym and taught volleyball skills and played a game.

11. Watercolor: the student showed a powerpoint about different artists and then passed out paper, paint and water. She had students paint the flower arrangement she brought.

12. Cooking: the student brought ingredients to make cookies and brought the students to the home economics room to make the cookies.

13. Hair: the student talked about different hair products and showed how she styles hair. She then gave each student some fake hair and taught them how to braid.

14. ASL: the student presented a powerpoint about American sign language and then taught the students some sign language.

15. Air Force Junior Officer Training Course (AFJROTC): the student brought in artifacts from AFJROTC and a friend. They demonstrated marching and how to wear the uniform.

Depending on the mentee's language levels, I have also offered for mentees to teach a class. Oftentimes, because the mentee has limited English, they are not ready to teach for a whole period, but I have had EL student mentees teach for 5–10 minutes.

This activity proved to be a favorite of many students because they get to learn about various topics and because many students love being able to lead the class. Students gain confidence through peer teaching, mostly due to the fact that the students in the class are so welcoming and attentive. Peer teaching can happen in any classroom, with any grade.

## Additional Activities

In addition to the previous activities mentioned in this chapter, partners work together on the following activities:

### My New Home Presentation

A representative from the local tourism agency comes to the class and presents about the history, demographics and places around the city. Next, students use a graphic organizer to gather more information about the city. It is important to create a graphic organizer that lists the main idea of each section and how many pieces of evidence they need. Mentors help facilitate the research and help mentees use technology and teach them appropriate ways to cite research on the graphic organizer. Students then use Google Slides to record their research and add pictures. Students then practice reading through the slideshow with their partners. When finished, mentees and mentors present to the class together.

### Communication Games

**Drawing Blind**: Students sit back-to-back, so they cannot see each other. Each student has a paper and pencil. One student gets a picture card with a scene on it from the teacher. The student then starts describing the scene on the card to the other student. The student listening tries to draw the scene as the other student describes. This game takes a lot of verbal communication and students are always surprised at how hard it is to not use any other of their senses to communicate.

**Walking Blind**: Students are given a list of places around the school and head into the hallway with one blindfold per partner group. Their mission is to lead their partner to each place with only their voice. One student puts on the blindfold and the other student stands behind him/her. The students are allowed to only use their voices to help guide their partner. They give each other commands like "go five steps forward" and "take two side steps to the right." Once the student makes his/her way to the first place, the partners switch roles and continue to the next place on the list. The teacher should also go into the hallways and watch the students as they make their way around the school.

## Traditions

**Carving Pumpkins**: Throughout the year, students participate in many activities related to traditions and cultures. One activity students partake in is pumpkin carving. This is usually the first time my EL students carve a pumpkin. We watch a video about the history of pumpkin carving and students draw out a picture of what they want to carve on the pumpkin. Then students head into the home economics room, with a sink and non-carpeted floor. There, they each have a pumpkin to carve. Beforehand, I buy the pumpkins, find some old newspapers and borrow knives, spoons and bowls from the home economics teacher. Students bond over digging out the slimy insides and carving funny faces together.

**Holidays**: Students learn about a variety of different holidays. For example, students learn about the Muslim holiday of Ramadan, the Nepali holiday of Daishan, Vietnamese and Chinese New Year and Christmas. For each holiday, students who celebrate the holiday share their experiences and present games, food or activities that they do during that holiday.

## Project-Based Learning With Global Goals

In addition to learning about traditions and cultures, students engage in project-based learning pertaining to the 17 United Nations Sustainable Development Goals (UNSDGs). It is essential that teachers encourage advocacy and empower students to be global citizens that take action. Since I work to cultivate a classroom of empathetic learners. I am aware of how culture influences behavior. I believe that the world is my classroom. There are no boundaries, no walls. Students need to learn from teachers, who are themselves, global citizens.

In 2019, I traveled to Greece and met an inspiring Greek teacher named Aggeliki Pappa. A veteran educator, she started a school for dyslexic Greek students to learn English. Her style of teaching involves active learning and theater, all while encouraging her students to be global citizens. A global project that she created is called the SOS4Love project. The project stands for "Students Organize Solutions" and promotes the SDGs and love. It uses an online platform for students to connect and share a goal they wish to accomplish related to the SDGs.

In the fall of 2019, my mentors and mentees chose one SDG to focus on. Students were able to virtually talk to Aggeliki about her work and the goals. They also participated in her project and committed to taking action on one of the goals. I thought that it was important to educate our whole school about the SDGs, so I created a SDG poster project. Local community activists visited the class and students researched their chosen SDG to create an action plan. Mentors and mentees worked together and created large posters for each SDG and hung them throughout the school. Next, I set up a contest to raise awareness and had it broadcasted on the morning announcements for two weeks. While creating the posters, my students included a QR code on each, so that students could scan the code to enter the school-wide SDG contest. The QR code directed students to a Google form where they would record their name and what they could do to take action on the SDG. The students who had entered an answer for all seventeen posters were entered to win one of four $25 gift cards to the local grocery store. In addition, some students also presented their projects on each of the SDGs to elementary students at the end of the year. My students were the first in the school to address global citizenship through SDGs. The idea of using QR codes and posters in the hallways to facilitate learning and promote awareness could actually be done with a multitude of topics and projects.

While my students were initially learning about the SDG pertaining to clean water, I created an obstacle course in the gym for students. Students had to hold a jug of water in each hand while they stopped to gather food, change clothes, tend to children (dolls) and avoid dangers such as rivers, animals and injuries. My EL students, who had been used to carrying water for long distances, performed the course with ease, while the other students complained at how heavy the water was. After the activity, the EL students talked about the different ways they got water in their native countries. The non-EL students were fascinated by the fact that water didn't just come out of a facet for everyone. One of the EL students even showed everyone how she could carry five gallons of water at one time from one end of the gym to the other. At the end of class, I assigned all of the mentor students to carry around a gallon of water, with the SDG logo on it, for 24 hours. They had to bring it everywhere they went. They also had to explain what the SDGs were to anyone that asked. The main objective of the activity was for the students to understand what it felt like to always have to think about water. Most of them never thought about where water came from or what would happen if they didn't have access to water. My EL students and many others around the world know what it is like to have to worry about not having access to clean drinking water. There are many other activities that teachers can do in their classrooms to help students understand the SDGs and what it means to be a global citizen.

Any teacher can use the SDGs as tools to teach about sustainable development and the world we live in. I know many teachers who teach using the Global Goals in their classrooms.

◆ A high school English teacher in Utah uses the Global Goals as the topics for persuasive essays.

- ◆ An elementary teacher in New Jersey partners with a teacher from Tennessee to bring their classes together, working on projects pertaining to the goals.
- ◆ A fourth-grade teacher had her students write books about the goals and then shared them with their kindergarten buddies.
- ◆ A high school home economics teacher uses the Global Goal pertaining to hunger to explore topics of food waste and food insecurity.

## We Are America

*As a little girl, I adored playing with Barbies and sneaking into my mom's room and taking her makeup. Living in Bosnia, I had some struggles and I wasn't accepted by the way I looked or dressed because I had a very different style than others. I was born in America, but my parents moved us to their native country when I was in second grade. The mean comments other people made about the way I looked became a normal thing. Sometimes I felt lonely, even though I had friends. It was hard to relate to anyone. Emina Sabanovic.*

*(We Are America Fargo, 2020)*

One of the most memorable projects that I worked on with my PNA students was the We Are America project. This was another opportunity to help amplify my students' voices by teaching empathy while engaging and empowering them. During the 2019–2020 school year, I had the pleasure of connecting with Jessica Lander, EL teacher and author from Massachusetts. She received a grant as a Bush Fellow and created the national We Are America project. The concept was similar to my Journey to America project, to share student voices. Her project, however, was open to educators across the country. Any middle or high school teacher, with any population, could apply to be a part of the year-long project to help students write stories about something important to them. The purpose was to start a national conversation around what it means to be American. She provided a curriculum that took educators through the project from brainstorming, all the way to publishing. The curriculum created by the We Are America staff focuses on empathy, empowerment and vulnerability. The contacts for the curriculum are some of Jessica's former students who work with the project as well. I found that as the project progressed, students became more comfortable with sharing their thoughts and experiences. It was a powerful dynamic to have EL students work together in partnership with their mentors during this project. Students were enthralled with each other's stories. After students had finished their final drafts, which were two pages double spaced, I took a portrait of each student and sent everything to Jessica and her team. They did the layout and sent the proof back. After editing the proof, I had students record their voices while reading their stories and sent those and the proof back again. In the end, the students' portraits and audios of their stories were featured on the We Are America website and Jessica sent us 125 professionally bound *We Are America Fargo* books, covered by the grant, for the students and community to share.

One of my favorite parts of the project was when students read a rough draft of their stories out loud for the first time in our sharing circle. There was laughter, tears and excitement. The We Are America Project certainly helped to create empathy and engage my students, empowering them to share their stories and advocate for themselves. There is a new cohort of teachers who do the project each year. If you teach middle or high schools students, you can learn more about the project at https://www.weareamericaproject.com/about.

## Native Country Presentations

"Okay, but why do you wear that thing on your head?" a small first grader with freckles and long blonde braids asked.

"This? Oh, this is my hijab. I am Muslim, so in my religion, women wear this to maintain privacy and modesty," *Fara said with a smile. The small first grader looked at her curiously.

"It is kind of like a nun," Fara's mentor, *Jen added. "Has anyone seen a Catholic nun wearing a head covering?" A couple students raised their hands and some nodded. Fara and Jen continued with their presentation on Somalia, as the elementary students eagerly listened, fascinated by the powerpoint. After the lesson, Fara and Jen showed the students how to play traditional games that Fara played growing up in Somalia. The lesson ended with each student getting a sample of a sambusa, a Somalian baked pastry with vegetables and meat, that Fara and Jen had cooked together. Fara had invited Jen to her house the night before to cook over 50 sambusas for the elementary students.

For the final project of their PNA class, the students presented about the EL partner's native country at a local elementary school. An EL teacher at a local elementary school reached out to me and asked if any of my EL high school students wanted to present something for their school-wide diversity day. I took this opportunity and meshed it with the projects that my students were going to present to the class. Instead of just presenting in front of each other, the EL students and mentors had the unique opportunity to take on a teacher role and present to younger students. Not only did this help the EL students practice their English skills, but it also gave them a platform to teach others about their culture and traditions. This was important because our EL students often felt like many people didn't understand them due to language and cultural differences. The more people that could be educated about diversity, the better. Both partners also loved the idea of teaching younger students. The experience was different from teaching their peers. When they taught younger students, they were looked up to, because they were older. Many cultures around the world emphasize the importance of respecting elders, even if the elder was only five years older.

Partners worked together on the powerpoint presentation for weeks, researching and planning together. They were then tasked with taking on the role of "teachers" and creating a lesson plan that included a 15 minute interactive lesson and a ten-minute activity. I showed examples and videos from previous years and each partner group had to present a practice lesson to the class. Students prepared their activities the days leading up to the presentations. Activities had to be hands-on, with elementary students in mind. They also had to be adapted for the different range of abilities, since varying grades of elementary classes would rotate through their presentations every 25 minutes. (*See LESSONS for example activities and Lesson details.*)

Mentors helped the EL students with the technical and language heavy parts of the project, all the while learning more about their own EL partners. "Wait, you had how many cows when you lived in Kenya?" *Kari asked *Ahmed.

"About 100 or so, sometimes I lost a couple. Lions would come at night and try to attack the cows, but when I would hear the lions, I would just try to scare them off with my fire," Ahmed replied. Kari stared at Ahmed for a second, to see if he was joking. He wasn't.

"So, weren't you scared?" Kari asked.

"No," Ahmed said with a smile. He curled up his bicep. "I am strong man!" By this time, the whole class had overheard the conversation and everyone started to giggle. Kari shared with me earlier how she could not believe how much responsibility Ahmed had to take on and how much tragedy that he had endured. "It sure does put things into perspective," she told me. Kari was born in a small, rural North Dakota town and moved to Fargo for high school. She had never interacted with anyone of a different religion or of a different race before starting high school. At the end of the year, she told me that she wished she would have taken the PNA class sooner, because she hadn't really ventured outside of her circle of White, U.S. born friends for the last four years. "With my partner in PNA, I learn something new everyday! I think I missed out on getting to know some really cool people during high school," she told me. This was the type of feedback that I received from all of the mentors. Mentors were surprised and enlightened by their mentees. EL students were equally surprised by their mentors. They were surprised that their mentors were so helpful and actually wanted to learn about them. They were surprised that when they saw their mentor in the hall, they would smile and wave. They were surprised to be invited to eat next to their mentors at the lunch table. They were surprised by such a welcoming environment.

You don't need to have an official class to help students create partnerships within your school, although it helps. Starting by assigning a buddy to a new EL student from day one, not just for the day but for the year, can make a huge difference. This is one connection that the new student makes right away. The idea is that this connection will give way to many more, as the buddy introduces the student to their friends. This is also the peer that the new student can go to with questions or concerns that they may be too shy to bring up during class or with a teacher. Where do you find reliable buddies? I have found that senior students seem to be the most reliable, for obvious reasons. In my experience, students who want to be teachers, those in student government, or theater seem to make great partners. In addition, if you know your new student played a sport or was in a certain activity, immediately connect them with other student players or a coach. I have seen how sports and activities have helped many students connect and gain a sense of belonging.

Another way to help new EL students is to connect your EL class with a mainstream class. If you are an EL teacher who teaches sheltered instruction, consider reaching out to a teacher who teaches mostly non-EL students. Suggest that your students do a joint project or activity. It could be as short as one day or as long as a couple weeks. If you are tasked with working with EL students as part of a pull-out program, consider arranging for a non-EL student or a former EL student of the same age to be present during that time. Depending on their ages, you could facilitate a conversation or interview between them, giving each student specific questions to answer. You could also ask the non-EL or former EL student to eat lunch with the new student or to help show them around school. In addition, platforms like Zoom have made partnering with classrooms around the U.S. or even in other countries relatively easy. I like to use Zoom breakout rooms for students to interview each other and share about themselves. Flipgrid is another great platform that can be used to connect your students with others around the world.

## Concluding Thoughts

Partnerships amongst students, no matter if they are EL, special needs, native born or gifted, need to happen within our schools. This is especially important now, at a time when our nation and communities are so divided. We as educators need to foster empathy and help our students connect with each other. This way, they will be more likely to engage with those who are different from themselves, while feeling empowered to advocate for a more equitable, just and sustainable world.

> *"Overall, this class was very eye opening to me. It taught me more about the students I walk amongst everyday at school. It also helped me to open up to new students more. I will take what others have taught me about the lives of new Americans with me throughout life. You never know what someone has been through by looking at them, and I wish more people would understand that and take the time to get to know others. I am genuinely thankful for the opportunity to be a part of a class like this, and I hope other students take the chance to do the same."*
>
> **-Partnership Class Mentor**

 ## Reflection Questions

1. How can you create partnerships in your classroom? School? Community?
2. What activities can you do to help students get to know each other better?
3. Does your school have a program that helps orientate new EL students to the school and community?
4. How can you help your students share their stories?
5. What have you done to help connect your students with the global community?

*Names in this chapter have been changed.

# LESSON EXAMPLES

## Native Country Presentation

Directions: You will be researching information about your home country. First, you will research and gather information about your home country, then you will be making a google slides presentation (10 mins) about your home country. Finally, you will come up with an activity for the students (10 mins)

The following is a list of information that is needed. Check off when done.

- ☐ EACH SLIDE SHOULD HAVE AT LEAST 2 PICTURES
- ☐ At least 1 video somewhere in the presentation (only 1–2 minute video)

   - ☐ 1. Name of the Home Country with names of the presenters
   - ☐ 2. Location & Climate of the Country (What continent?)
   - ☐ 3. Description of Wildlife (animals)
   - ☐ 4. Description of Two Landforms (Well-known mountains, rivers, deserts, etc.)
   - ☐ 5. Description of Vegetation (plants and trees)
   - ☐ 6. Description of Food
   - ☐ 7. Description of Languages Spoken
   - ☐ 8. Description of the School System
   - ☐ 9. Description of Culture (could include holidays, clothing, music, etc.)

DESCRIBE YOUR ACTIVITY—It should be 10 minutes and be interactive.

What is the activity?

What materials will you need?

## Google Slide Outline

1. Name of the Home Country with names of the presenters
2. Location & Climate of the Country (What continent?)

   A.
   B.
   C.

3. Description of Wildlife (animals)

   A.
   B.
   C.

4. Description of Two Landforms (well-known mountains, rivers, deserts, etc.)

   A.
   B.
   C.

5. Description of Vegetation (plants and trees)

   A.
   B.
   C.

6. Description of Food

   A.
   B.
   C.

7. Description of Languages Spoken

   A.
   B.
   C.

8. Description of the School System
9. Description of Culture (could include holidays, clothing, music, etc.)

# Native Country Example Organization

Note to coordinating elementary teacher: Every group will need to be able to project their slideshows on a computer. They will not be bringing computers, because theirs do not connect with projectors. I will share ALL google slideshows with you and you can share them with the appropriate teacher/classroom where they will be presenting. Many groups will need colors/markers for their coloring sheets, as noted below. I will also share a folder on google drive with you that has all the coloring/worksheets for the students so that you can make the number of copies you need.

| GROUP ACTIVITY MATERIALS | NEEDED (coloring sheet groups need colors/markers) |
|---|---|
| 1. Mexico- Slideshow on Mexico- Vocab, Bingo | Printed: Bingo cards, bingo markers or pencils |
| 2. China- Slide show-Chinese Language, color | Printed: Coloring language sheet |
| 3. Nepal- Holidays, food/tika on forehead | Printed in color: Money (cut out- each gets 1 dollar) |
| 4. Nepali- Dance-performed and then teach a dance to the kids | None |
| 5. Congo/Swahili- language, make bracelet | Need string, scissors & Beads: sky blue, red, yellow |
| 6. Bhutanese culture- slideshow, food, make flag | Printed: Flag coloring sheet, napkins |
| 7. African Dance- Dance show / kids dance | Need speaker for computer - YouTube |
| 8. Nepali Language- slideshow with videos | Printed: Coloring sheet with Nepali word |
| 9. Arabic Language- slideshow, alphabet sheet/coloring sheet | Printed: Coloring sheet with snake & Arabic alphabet |
| 10. Story readings- going from America (3 students) | Need Microphone |
| 11. Congo- google slide -African Dance | Need Speakers for computer |
| 12. Vietnam-google slide country/ dragon mask | Printed: Dragon mask, string, scissors |
| 13. Liberia- google slide country info/game/color flag | – Printed: Liberian flag color sheet |
| 14. Nepal- google slide about country, game | Need Marbles (40, if possible) |

(Continued)

| GROUP ACTIVITY MATERIALS | NEEDED (coloring sheet groups need colors/markers) |
|---|---|
| 15. Kenya- slide show, game | None |
| 16. Somalia- slide show, dance, food | Need: Napkins |
| 17. Eritrea- country slide show, make bracelet | Need: Beads (green, red, yellow, light blue), string, scissors |

# Native Country Teaching Lesson Plan

### Group 1 Somalia
Objective:
*Students will understand information about country of Somalia*
Activity 1

Google Slide show about the traditions, land and people of Somalia.

Activity 2

Show an example of a traditional Dance
Have students practice and then try it with us
Pass out traditional food—called Mandazi
Have students try on Somali Clothes
Materials needed—clothes, food, napkins, music, ppt

### Vietnam Group 2
Objective:
*Students will understand about the country of Vietnam and Vietnamese traditions*
Activity 1

Google Slide show about Vietnam

Activity 2

Hand out materials and students will color dragon masks
(*Facilitator will find a dragon outline from internet*)

Materials needed-
Dragon' face picture
Color pencils
Scissors
Strings

### NEPAL Group 3
Objective:
*Students will understand: Students will understand the basic words of Nepali and will be able to say it. And also know the phrases of greetings*

Activity 1 We will teach them Nepali alphabet, colors, and numbers.

Activity 2 We will teach them Nepali greeting words and let the students color the outline drawing of the Mt. Everest....

Materials needed—We need the Mount. Everest image and number on top and five alphabet's on top also and colors.

## Reference

Juelke, L. (Ed.). (2020). *We Are America Fargo*. The We Are America Project.

**Part 3**

# Critical Components for Developing a Welcoming Program for English Learners

*By Sarahí Monterrey*

# 7

# Building Relationships With Families

As the dates for parent-teacher conferences each school year approached, I heard the same conversation over and over between my mother and my father. My dad would tell my mom the date for the parent-teacher conference and ask, "¿Vamos? (Let's go?)" My mom would always respond, "Yo no, ve tú. ¡Yo no entiendo nada! (Not me, you go. I don't understand anything!)"

I witnessed this routine from elementary school through high school. My dad was always the one to attend parent-teacher conferences with my brothers and me because my mom did not feel comfortable going. Immigrating to the United States in their mid-twenties from El Salvador, having to learn English, yet feeling like their English was not good enough. Learning how the U.S. educational system functioned brought some anxiety to my parents, especially my mother. Despite the anxiety, my dad would attend parent-teacher conferences, but he could never convince my mom to go.

When I became an English Language Learner teacher, I constantly thought of my parents' experience as immigrant parents. I made it a priority to build strong relationships with families, to ensure that they felt welcomed, and as a school community, to engage them in their child's educational journey. Research has shown that high parental involvement has a significant impact on youth, especially Latino youth (Alexander et al., 2017).

DOI: 10.4324/9781003177333-11

In my 18-year career as a teacher, I have witnessed firsthand the powerful impact of building strong relationships with families.

When students know that their teachers communicate with their families regularly and that their parents/guardians feel comfortable contacting the school with any concerns, the level of accountability and success for that student rises exponentially. I had students who used to skip classes, but they quickly learned that it would be difficult to get away with skipping because I would immediately call home to inquire about their absence.

Just this week, I had a student ask me, "Mrs. Monterrey, why do you call our parents when we skip school?" I responded, "Because I care about your education. Being present in school is important for your success. I know your parents/guardians would like to know if you are not here at school. I like working with your families as a team to make sure you are successful and graduate high school." When students see educators and parents working as a team to ensure their success, it can make all the difference in the world for that student. It sends a strong message to that student that they matter. Whenever I call home to speak with a parent or guardian about any concern or when I call to share great news about their child's academic progress, they are always so appreciative of the communication. It is crucial to communicate with families in the language spoken at home to ensure they clearly understand the information shared.

## Essential Elements to Build Strong Relationships With EL Families

A question I often get asked is, "How do we build relationships with English Learner (EL) families so that they can be engaged and feel a part of the school community?" One of the essential aspects of engaging families is clear communication. Schools must evaluate their communication systems and determine if all communication elements are accessible to EVERY family by providing translation/interpretation in the families' native language. Whether it is communication through emails, automated calls, newsletters, letters being mailed home or communicating at parent-teacher conferences, etc., the question needs to be asked, what systems are in place at our school to ensure that the information is accessible to families who do not speak English?

It is essential to know our school's demographics to determine the families' language needs. In the school districts where I have taught, most EL families speak Spanish as their native language. Since I am also a native Spanish speaker, it has been advantageous for me and has facilitated communication with families. However, many districts have many different languages spoken by EL families. As a result, ensuring that information is accessible to every family becomes more challenging.

In districts where many different languages are spoken, a good approach to take would be to identify interpretation/translation services that can be used to help facilitate communication. For example, a couple of years ago, I was working with a family from Vietnam. Although the parents spoke some English and we were able to communicate effectively in most cases, there were a couple of meetings where we used an interpretation agency. We had a professional Vietnamese interpreter on a conference call to ensure accurate communication with the family. I have also worked with several Burmese families from Myanmar whose native language is Karen. When communicating with our Burmese families, we have worked with their church sponsors, who have done a fantastic job serving as their advocates.

It is also vital to keep in mind what systems are put in place so that families can contact the school and communicate their needs if they do not speak English. Whether they need to report an absence, get information about sporting events, or any other reason, having a system in place for parents to communicate their needs to school personnel is critical. As an EL teacher, I have always viewed advocacy for families and students as a vital part of my role. Often, advocating for families requires having conversations with administrators to build their knowledge of English Learners and their family's needs. Bringing principals on board to ensure that systems are put in place to guarantee communication is accessible for families who do not speak English is paramount.

About ten years ago, my district changed the phone system and implemented a feature where our classroom phones would not receive any calls from outside our building so that instruction would not be interrupted when teachers are teaching. When I was informed about this change, I was immediately concerned about how this would impact communication with families who regularly called me with any concerns about school, to report an absence, pick up their child early from school or any other need. I met with the principal and asked if we could leave the phone in the EL classroom with the capability to accept calls from outside of our building. I was surprised when the initial response was, "Why would you want your phone ringing during class?" I had to explain that our school did not have any bilingual staff members in the office, and if a family were to call, communication could be a barrier. I also explained that the EL department worked extremely hard to develop trusting relationships with families and to create an environment where families felt comfortable contacting the EL staff.

After explaining how the new system would negatively impact communication with bilingual families, the principal allowed our phone to be one of the few classrooms in the school with the capability of accepting phone calls from outside of our building. This experience is an example of how procedures and systems may be put into place without considering multilingual families' language needs. As EL teachers, we bring a language lens that others may not have. We must advocate for families so that they have the access they need to our schools.

## The Power of a Bilingual Parent Group

Many times, educators may think that EL families are not concerned with their child's education and do not care to attend school events, but that could not be farther from the truth. Most families wish they could be more involved but see language as a barrier that deters them from attending school events. A strategy that I have found to be impactful in building relationships with families and engaging them in their child's educational journey has been creating a bilingual parent group.

In 2002, while working on my final project for my master's degree, I decided to strive to increase parental engagement by implementing a bilingual parent group. It was my second year of teaching, and I spent the previous year getting to know families and focused a lot of my energy on building systems of communication. By the second year, I had established trust and a rapport with families where they felt welcomed and comfortable coming to school. I also had the opportunity to co-teach with an English teacher who was also passionate about working with English Language Learners and their families. I shared my idea with her of creating a bilingual parent group, and she was eager to collaborate and get it started. We decided to personally call families to share with them the idea of a bilingual parent group. Overwhelmingly, the families responded with eagerness and excitement about establishing a group for bilingual parents where meetings would be held in Spanish and focus on addressing their needs. Our goal was to empower parents by opening an avenue for them to feel connected to our school and give them a voice through a bilingual parent group.

An essential aspect of implementing a parent group is using a funds of knowledge framework where families are viewed as partners and allowed to share their strengths and knowledge to work collaboratively to provide their child the necessary support to experience success (Protacio et al., 2021). At our first meeting, our goal was to foster an environment where parents felt they had a voice and stressed that their interests and needs would guide the group. Collectively, we determined how often we would meet, for how long and what the topic should be for each meeting. Empowering families by giving them a voice and fostering an equal partnership environment was instrumental in the parent group's success. After each meeting, I always had parents say that the group members decided that we would meet monthly. The topics they chose varied from how to check students' grades and academic progress to effective strategies parents can use to support learning at home, to taking a tour of the public library and learning about the services the library has to offer. It was invigorating to see the way parents were engaged and excited to be at school. Through the parent group, families were able to get to know other families, and it led to a community of parents that now felt supported and had a sense of belonging. "¡Muchas gracias, Maestras! Estas reuniones son excelentes y aprendemos tanto. (Thank you, teachers! These meetings are excellent and we learn so much.)"

The bilingual parent group had such a positive impact on building strong relationships with English Learners' families that when I moved to my current district, one of my goals was to create a bilingual parent group there. Two key takeaways from my first experience in creating a parent group that I made sure to follow are: (1) do not feel like you have to do it alone. Find colleagues who are as passionate about this work and are eager to collaborate with you; and (2) establish a shared partnership where parents play an instrumental role in guiding the group.

I was fortunate to have a colleague, Edna Maldonado, in the EL department in my current district who was eager to join me in bringing the parent group to life. An advantage of the second parent group we created was that the advancements in technology made it even easier to reach families and maintain regular communication with the group. We created a closed Facebook group where we posted information about our meetings, important events happening at school and even pictures of our EL students' participating in exciting activities. We also used the Remind App as another tool to facilitate communication, and parents rave about how helpful the Remind App is.

I find myself constantly evaluating situations and examining areas where we can improve communication. The Remind App has been instrumental in improving our communication with families for our parent group and overall communication regarding important information in our school. For example, our school began using an automated all-call system more regularly to inform families when we had a lockdown drill, reminders about parent-teacher conferences or other essential information. After the all-calls were made, I regularly received phone calls from families stating they did not understand what the message said since it was all in English. It occurred to me that with the Remind App, I could easily send families a transcribed message in their native language containing the same information as the all-call. I set up a meeting with the principal and explained that many families who did not speak English were calling me because they did not understand the message in the all-calls that were being made. I asked her if we could implement a system where I would be informed when all-calls would be made and if I could be given the message beforehand so that I could send families the information in their native language through the Remind App.

As soon as we put this system in place, we noticed a significant difference. Instead of families calling me to tell me they were confused and did not understand the message, families messaged in the Remind App, thanking me for the communication. One of the Remind App's most valuable features is that when sending a message, there is a globe at the left-hand side of the message box, and when selected, you can have the message translated in many different languages. This feature is beneficial in districts where EL families speak many different languages. I tested the translation feature in Spanish to assess the translation quality and was impressed with the translation provided.

Although technology has been transformational in the way we communicate with families, we cannot make assumptions about a parent or guardian's abilities to use technology. Some feel entirely comfortable using email, Facebook groups, and various apps, but others expressed needing training on using these various platforms. During one of our parent group meetings, we taught families how to use the technology platform (Infinite Campus) used in our school for accessing grades and an app our district uses called School Messenger. We showed them how to request being added to our Facebook group and did a tutorial on how to use the Remind App. A few parents did not have email accounts, and we even helped them set up their email. Equipping families with valuable skills such as these help them feel empowered and contributes significantly to improving communication and building relationships with families.

One of the most challenging aspects of creating a bilingual parent group is determining the best time to meet. With busy schedules, it is nearly impossible to find a time that works for everyone. During the first meeting, we surveyed families to get their input on a meeting time and day of the week that would work best for them. The most vital aspect of scheduling meetings for the parent group is consistency. Our meetings were on the second Wednesday of every month from 6:00 to 7:00 pm. Having consistency has been imperative in having many families come consistently to our meetings. The table below includes the various topics we have covered during our meetings, which were all chosen collaboratively with parents to ensure we addressed their interests, questions and concerns.

Giving parents a voice and having them be decision-makers on what is covered during our meeting is of utmost importance. A couple of years ago, an idea came up from the parent group to explore a way for parents to share with the rest of the teachers in our school about their background and the challenges they face with parental involvement. Although the parent group helped EL families feel more connected to our school, there was still a communication gap with the rest of the teachers.

To address this gap, we created a video where families could express themselves to teachers and share what they wish teachers knew about them. I shared the idea with a friend who had a connection with someone who worked for the local Telemundo station. Thankfully, two videographers volunteered to help us with this video project. The prompts that guided the video interviews were:

1. Tell us about yourself and the dreams and aspirations you have for your children and family.
2. What would you like teachers to know about the importance of education in your family?
3. How does the language barrier impact your ability to be involved in the school?
4. Is there anything that teachers can do so that you feel more connected to the school?
5. Is there something else that you wish teachers knew about you/your child or your family?

We were able to record the video over the summer, which included three families. That fall, we shared the video during a staff meeting. Staff members commented on how valuable the insight that these families provided was for them. This is another example of how parents were given the space to have a voice and feel heard through the bilingual parent group. If you would like to watch the video, it can be accessed on YouTube at the following web address: https://youtu.be/LGBdutpytNc

---

*Parent Group Topics*

- Who are our EL teachers?
  - We give a handout with contact information for the EL teachers at our school and district EL department personnel during the first meeting.
- What is the purpose of the bilingual parent group?
- How to report attendance
- Overview of our school's weekly schedule
- Communication:
  - Robocalls, Remind App, School Messenger App and Facebook Private Group
- How to use Infinite Campus to check grades
  - Login and passwords
- Requirement and process for free and reduced lunch
- What is ACCESS testing?
- District Graduation Requirements
- What is the process to apply to college?
- What are Scholarships & Financial Aid?
- FAFSA Night
- Registering for summer school
- Summer Pre-College Programs
- School Safety—What are the different drills conducted at school? What measures are taken to ensure safety at school?
- Overview of the ACT
- Services offered at our public library
- How to recognize signs of drug/substance use in teens

---

## Hosting a FAFSA Night

One of my favorite events that stemmed from the bilingual parent group was hosting a Free Application for Federal Student Aid (FAFSA) night. Completing the FAFSA form can be a daunting experience for any family. When you add a language barrier and questions about varying family dynamics, overwhelming does not begin to describe most families' feelings. To help ease the anxiety of the FAFSA process, I created a FAFSA night at our school. Although there are events held at universities throughout Wisconsin to help families complete the FAFSA, most times, there are no interpreters present. There is also some hesitation from families to discuss such personal financial information in a place where they do not know the staff. By having the FAFSA night at our school, we provided a place where families already felt safe and with whom they already built a relationship with and trust.

To set up the FAFSA night, I contacted financial aid advisors from our local universities. I asked if they would be willing to assist us in our FAFSA night by being present to help guide families as they completed the online FAFSA application. We had five financial aid advisors join us and our district's family liaison, counselors and EL staff. Although not all of the financial aid advisors were bilingual, we had enough bilingual staff members who helped with interpretation. I reserved two of our computer labs, and the financial aid advisors and district staff circulated between the two labs. The energy during this event was so positive it was refreshing to experience it. Families felt relieved and excited to leave that night knowing their FAFSA application was complete and done with professional staff support.

Although the first year of the FAFSA night was designed for families in the EL department, it was such a success that we decided to open our school's FAFSA night to all families of seniors. It was gratifying to see an idea that stemmed from our bilingual parent group develop into an event that impacts our larger school community.

## How to Create a Bilingual Parent Group

I cannot stress enough the difference that a bilingual parent group can make in building strong relationships with families, which leads to a more robust support system for students and positively impacts their academics. For educators interested in implementing a bilingual parent group at their school, I recommend starting with a careful analysis of the EL program's demographics. What are the home languages of the families at the school? If there are multiple languages spoken, who are individuals available to support interpreting at meetings? Are there interpreting agencies that can provide interpreters? Although working with more than one language group can be a challenge, I recommend using as many strategies and tools as possible to include all languages spoken.

It is also critical to find a time and day of the week that works for most parents and be consistent with the monthly meetings. Be sure to use a funds of knowledge framework to create an environment where families feel they are partners on this journey and have a voice. Take the time to listen to what their concerns and needs are. Let the ideas come about organically from families, and you will witness what a transformational experience having a bilingual parent group can be.

## Concluding Thoughts

Taking the time to be strategic and purposeful in engaging families in the school community will benefit all stakeholders. It will allow educators to learn more about each family, their backgrounds and valuable insight that may help address students' needs more efficiently. It gives families a sense of belonging, an opportunity to have a "go-to" person at the school and to learn valuable information regarding the educational system that they may find helpful as they seek ways to support their child's learning at home. For students, it lets them know that they have adults working together in their best interest for them to have the best educational experience possible. For administrators, it brings to light the need to ensure an inclusive school community for EVERY family by having systems in place that foster two-way communication. The time and energy invested in building strong relationships with families are well worth it!

 ## Reflection Questions

1. What can you do to make families of English Learners feel welcome at school?
2. What systems are in place at your school to provide families with information in their native language?

3. What do you do to foster open communication with families?
4. How can you get input and feedback from families about the types of supports they need to support their child's education?
5. How can you empower families to have a voice at your school?

## References

Alexander, J. D., Cox, R. B. Jr., Behnke, A., & Larzelere, R. E. (2017). Is all parental "noninvolvement" equal? Barriers to involvement and their relationship to Latino academic achievement. *Hispanic Journal of Behavioral Sciences*, *39*(2), 169–179.

Protacio, M. S., Piazza, S. V., & David, V. (2021). Family engagement in the middle: Reaching out to families of English Learners. *Middle School Journal*, *52*(1), 30–39.

# 8

# Building Staff Capacity

In Spanish, there is a famous saying, "En la unión está la fuerza." This phrase translates to, "In unity is where the strength lies." This saying has played an instrumental role in my life because I often think, "What can I do to help my community?"

I decided to become an English Learner (EL) teacher because I often heard of the high dropout rates of Latinx students from a young age. I also reflected on my education and realized that in all of my K-12 education, I only had two Latinx teachers; Mr. Hernandez, my kindergarten teacher and Señor Furio, my high school Spanish teacher. I felt a calling to become a high school EL teacher with the hopes of inspiring students to dream big, graduate and feel prepared for their life journey beyond high school.

It is no secret that the U.S. teaching profession is mainly made up of white teachers and does not accurately reflect our students' diversity. In Wisconsin, the disproportionality is vast, with 91% of teachers being white despite only 70% of students. For years, the population of English Learners in the United States has continued to grow. However, despite the continued growth, many teachers do not feel prepared to utilize effective instruction that supports English Learners' academic development. This is due to a lack of emphasis on ELs in teacher preparation programs (Flores et al., 2015).

ELs walk into classrooms every day and receive instruction from teachers that feel ill-equipped to address their language

DOI: 10.4324/9781003177333-12

and academic needs. Therefore, it is imperative to build staff capacity to work with English learners by building their knowledge on challenges that English learners face, providing them with strategies and best practices in serving ELs, and establishing a culture of collaboration and support between the English learner department and content teachers to foster shared responsibility for addressing the needs of English Learners (Hadjioannou et al., 2016). I firmly believe that the more teachers collaborate, the more significant impact we can have on students and our school communities. Our strength lies in unity and collaborating.

## Setting Teachers up for Success With English Learners

It was the fall of 2004, after teaching in the town where I graduated college from, I felt it was time to move back to my Wisconsin hometown so I could be closer to relatives. I was able to get a teaching position in a neighboring town as a Spanish teacher.

As I started my new teaching position and attended our first staff meeting, I immediately noticed that, once again, I was the only teacher of color on the entire staff. Word quickly spread amongst the roughly 25 Latinx students that there was a Latinx teacher at school. Although I didn't have any of them in my classes because I was teaching beginning level Spanish classes, they regularly visited my classroom. I quickly discovered that many of them were failing classes. Some students did not speak English, and the school did not offer any services for ELs. It was a sink or swim model. I often helped students with homework after school.

After multiple meetings without any support from administration to design proper programming and exhausting all possibilities to find a solution, I made one of the toughest decisions I have ever made and resigned. This was a difficult decision because I felt I was letting students down. I was torn.

This was clearly an issue of equity. These students were not receiving the services they needed to experience academic success. I could not stay in a district that was not aligned with my values and beliefs. What saddens me is that issues of equity are prevalent in schools all across our nation and have plagued our public school system since its existence. Unfortunately, the ones who suffer the consequences are students who do not end up reaching their full potential.

The following school year, I returned to the district where I first started teaching to continue developing the EL program at the high school. Going through this experience was a wake-up call of how critical it is for EL teachers to advocate for appropriate services and programming for ELs. I realized that not many administrators felt knowledgeable enough to ensure proper programming, and not many educators felt prepared to provide ELs the necessary instructional practices to address their academic needs.

Facing the reality that many teachers feel ill-equipped to address ELs' language and academic needs means that an English Learner teacher's role becomes even more valuable. As EL teachers, we are in a prime position to share our knowledge and build staff capacity. How EL teachers build staff capacity will vary depending on the dynamics at a particular school. However, there are essential elements that are critical to building staff capacity. A key element is to build staff knowledge around the demographics of EL students in our schools and the EL program model.

Many teachers outside of the EL department do not know the difference in program models or the makeup of the EL students in a particular school. To address this knowledge gap, at the beginning of the school year, I share valuable information with teachers pertaining to our EL students during our professional development week before classes begin. I share with teachers a list of our EL students (With the phonetic pronunciation of their names, each student's home language, and their English proficiency levels.), a Google folder with all of the Individualized Learning Plans (ILPs), a chart of World-Class Instructional Design and Assessment (WIDA's) "Can Do Descriptors" and include which EL teacher they should contact if they need additional information or support. I also share with staff a presentation in which I explain all of the information contained in the Google folder and our EL program's design at our school. Educators may need to approach administration to request time to provide all staff this essential information.

Many districts have recently started using Individualized Language Plans (ILPs). An ILP is a document that provides teachers a snapshot of an EL student and what services that student needs to experience success. The ILPs may contain a student's English proficiency level, language goals, anecdotal information and practical strategies/scaffolds needed for that particular student to develop their English skills. Providing teachers with the ILP of EL students in their classes and helping them understand how the ILP can be used to guide instruction can have a significant impact on ELs. However, it is imperative to provide staff training on what an ILP is and how to use them in a meaningful way. If a school district does not currently use ILPs and would like to explore incorporating them, there are many samples available on the web.

Explaining the program model and services provided is essential so that the staff understand the critical role they play in working together as a school community to address the needs of ELs. For example, Wisconsin is part of the WIDA consortium, which is made up of 40 U.S. states, territories and federal agencies dedicated to supporting English Language Learners in K-12 contexts (WIDA, n.d.). As a result of being part of the WIDA consortium, Wisconsin uses the ACCESS Test, which is designed by WIDA to determine students' English proficiency using a scale of 1–6. Our school uses sheltered ESL classes for students with English proficiency levels 1–2.9. There are also content classes that are co-taught by an EL teacher and a content area teacher. Additionally, there are other content classes where a push-in model is used, but due to not having a common prep to co-plan, the class is supported by an EL teacher instead of co-taught. We also have a class where EL students learn about study skills, life skills and receive support to increase achievement in their academic classes.

By building staff knowledge about the EL program in our schools, we highlight the significance of EL programs and place much needed emphasis on ensuring quality programming for ELs. As EL educators, we play a pivotal role in empowering teachers by providing them with valuable information needed to be purposeful and intentional in planning and making any needed shifts in instruction to improve achievement for ELs.

## Providing Staff Professional Development

To determine the areas in which teachers would like to receive more professional development to improve their practice in addressing ELs' academic needs, I administer a staff survey. Through this survey, teachers can have a voice and express what type of PD is needed for them to feel equipped to address ELs' needs in their classrooms. After examining the staff's needs, EL teachers should work with administrators to discuss when and how to offer professional development. I have had the opportunity to collaborate with colleagues on the creation of various professional development sessions.

At one of the schools in which I taught early in my career, the population of ELs was beginning to grow. Many of the teachers did not have experience working with ELs, which resulted in the professional development sessions focused on building staff's basic understanding of the terminology used when working with ELs. Staff learned about WIDA, what the different levels of English proficiency mean and how to use WIDA's "Can Do Descriptors."

One of the most impactful professional development sessions, where a significant number of staff members expressed how valuable the learning was, involved three valuable components: (1) A panel of EL students where students got to share with teachers what it is like being an English learner and how teachers can support their learning. (2) A panel of parents where families shared their hopes and dreams for their child and the challenges, they face in supporting their child's education. (3) An immersion experience in the shoes of an EL. I conducted a ten-minute mini-lesson in Spanish, knowing that most of the staff did not speak Spanish. I had the staff complete several tasks without providing any scaffolds. After the ten-minute mini-lesson, we discussed what it felt like being in the "shoes" of an EL student by engaging in a lesson where they had difficulty understanding the language. The immersion experience was eye-opening for many staff members, leading to many teachers making shifts in their teaching practices.

In 2016, immigration became a significant issue receiving much media coverage because of the change in administration in our country. A teacher asked our principal if our staff could receive professional development on immigration policies. The teacher knew some information about immigration but wanted to learn more about how immigration policies impact students. I had recently attended a workshop on immigration policies with my principal and one of our school counselors. When the idea of a Professional Development (PD) session on immigration policies was presented to my principal, she immediately thought to ask the counselor who attended the workshop with me and me if we would be willing to create a PD session for our staff using our learning from the workshop.

The PD included terminology related to immigration, such as the differences between being undocumented, a refugee or a mixed-status family, where family members may include people with different citizenship or immigration statuses. We also discussed policies such as DACA that directly impact students. I started the session by acknowledging that immigration is a controversial topic and that our PD's purpose was not to discuss our personal beliefs about immigration but rather to learn about immigration policies and how they impact students, and about understanding what we as educators can do to ensure a safe learning environment for ALL students.

An example of an immigration related policy in our state that many of our teachers were not aware of is that Wisconsin is considered a lockout state. Due to being a lockout state, undocumented students are required to pay out-of-state tuition if they would like to attend any public university. Many staff members were shocked to learn this information.

Overwhelmingly, staff expressed how valuable the PD was because they did not realize how much immigration policies affected many of our students and families. The two tables below include the information that I provided on the last two slides of my presentation, which I adapted from the presentation titled *Supporting Immigrant Students & Families Training for Educators* provided by neaedjustice.org.

---

*What Can Educators Do?*

- Be observant and establish trust—create an environment in which students feel safe.
- Be an active listener to see what a student might need.
- Be patient. Some students may exhibit behaviors and emotions that you have not seen before. Consider this when enforcing rules and other disciplinary actions.
- Be aware of your own bias and assumptions.
- Be cognizant of material used in your classroom that may increase anxiety.
- Recognize the importance of language. Teachers and other school personnel should be sensitive in their use of language, favoring terminology such as "undocumented/unauthorized immigrants" and making known that use of the terms "illegals" or "illegal immigrants/aliens" will not be tolerated in their classrooms. "Illegal alien" is not a legal term and is not an accurate descriptor as the status of being present in the U.S. without a visa is not actually a criminal violation. More importantly, these terms can have a dehumanizing impact by effectively rendering the individual and their entire existence as "illegal."
- Show your support. Teachers can demonstrate their support through images showing that they are allies. For example, Favianna Rodriguez's painting has become symbolic of the DREAMers movement: By displaying this on a whiteboard or desk, students are more likely to know that you are a "safe" person with whom they can discuss their immigration status-related stress.
- Communicate with your colleagues. Inform school staff (e.g., counselors, social workers, administration, ELL Teacher) regarding what you are seeing in the classroom so that appropriate services can be developed and needs can be addressed.

---

There have been other instances where the staff has requested PD on strategies to make content comprehensible for ELs. When providing staff with PD on strategies, it is vital to provide strategies that are practical and can seamlessly be incorporated into instruction. An excellent approach to take is to also build on strategies that may already be utilized in our schools.

For example, I have taught at schools that use AVID (Advancement Via Individual Determination), and many AVID strategies can be highly beneficial for ELs. For example, AVID has many handouts with sentence frames that allow students to develop higher-level questions or provide sentence frames for participating in a discussion. The use of sentence frames has been proven to be helpful for ELs. Building off of the AVID strategies that teachers are already using and emphasizing which strategies will have the most significant impact on ELs can increase teachers' chances of implementing these beneficial strategies.

Providing staff professional development geared toward the needs they have expressed is critical in building their capacity to address ELs' needs. The table below includes some of the most effective best practice strategies that I have highlighted when providing teachers professional development on working with ELs.

*Best Practice Strategies to Support Learning for ELs*

| Strategy | Rational |
|---|---|
| Focus on Funds of Knowledge (Greenberg & Vélez-Ibáñez, 1992) | - Students walk into our classrooms with life experiences and assets that can enhance their learning.<br>- Get to know your student and what they know so that you can build off of their knowledge and skills. |
| Build background knowledge | - Ask questions or use tools such as a KWL (Know, Want to Know, Learned) Chart that allows you to determine what students already know. Build any gaps in background knowledge needed before delivery of a lesson. |
| Use Sentence Frames | - Using sentence frames allows students to have a model of the language expectations. |
| Chunking Content | - For complex concepts or long units, it is best to chunk the content into smaller sections so that students can focus on a small section at a time. |
| Gradual Release of Responsibility (Pearson & Gallagher, 1983) | - Using the Gradual Release of Responsibility framework fosters independence by providing modeling from the teacher in the "I Do" phase and allows students to practice as a group in the "We Do" leading to students working independently in the "You Do" phase. |
| Incorporate Culturally Relevant Materials | - Allow students to see themselves reflected in the content they are learning. Using culturally relevant materials increases engagement and demonstrates the value in diversity. |

*(Continued)*

| *Best Practice Strategies to Support Learning for ELs (Continued)* | |
|---|---|
| *Strategy* | *Rational* |
| Give Time to Talk | - The more students can use their speaking skills and interact with native English speakers to model the use of the language, the more language growth will occur. |
| Pre-teach Vocabulary | - Pre-teaching vocabulary is essential, especially in content-specific disciplines with vocabulary that students may not already know. |
| Use Lots of Visuals! | - The more visuals available to students, the more the content comes alive. The language barrier is significantly reduced. |

## Co-Teaching to Build Staff Capacity

Beyond professional development, schools can build staff capacity through the EL department program model. Various program models have been used across our nation to address ELs' academic needs. Some of these models include pullout, push-in support, sheltered classes, etc. (Sugarman, 2018). One model that has demonstrated great potential in building teacher capacity and improving ELs' academic outcomes is the co-teaching model (Beninghof & Leensvaart, 2016). The co-teaching model allows content teachers to learn how to provide scaffolds and implement best practice strategies for ELs from the EL teacher, and simultaneously, the EL teacher builds their knowledge by learning from the content teacher's expertise in regards to the content in their discipline.

For a co-teaching partnership to be successful, essential elements need to be present to accomplish the goal of raising student achievement. The first element is for both teachers to have the disposition to have shared responsibility in all aspects of the class. Both teachers need to be open to co-planning, co-grading and setting up the class structure collaboratively. If the disposition is not there from both teachers, it could be a bad experience for all involved. It is also vital for administrators to support the co-teaching model by providing teachers co-planning time. Having co-planning time is imperative to ensure the success of the co-teaching partnership.

I have had the opportunity to co-teach with numerous teachers throughout my career in servicing English Learners. When co-planning, I have shared my expertise regarding language acquisition and have brought the language and cultural lens perspective to lesson planning. When I think of the significance of emphasizing the language and cultural lens, I think of an experience I had in second grade.

One day, I was taking a test where the task was to put a series of sentences in chronological order. The question dealt with how to make scrambled eggs. Sounds easy, right? As I read through the sentences, one particular sentence just did not seem to fit in. It read, "Place the egg in a bowl." The problem with this was that in my Salvadoran household, we never did that step. I always saw my mother make scrambled eggs by standing right next to the stove and cracking the eggs directly onto the pan. Although I was only a seven-year-old little girl, I still remember the feeling when I got my test back and saw that I got that question wrong.

Was that question a true indicator of my ability to put steps in chronological order? Absolutely not! Now that I am an educator and am able to view this situation from a different lens, I know my teacher most likely was oblivious to the cultural implication of the question for me. Having a co-teaching partnership where an EL teacher can share their views from a language and cultural lens with the content teacher can help bridge the gap in understanding why an EL student may struggle with a concept or do things a certain way.

One year, I was co-teaching an English 10 class where we were co-planning to introduce the novel *The Kite Runner*. My co-teacher and I discussed that *The Kite Runner* presented an excellent opportunity to build students' knowledge around the experience of refugees. Although most of the students in our EL department came from Latin America, we have a small percentage of students from Burma who grew up in refugee camps in Thailand. A few years ago, some of our Burmese students recorded a video about their experience as refugees. I shared the video with my co-teacher, and we created a lesson around it. One of our Burmese students was in our class, and his face lit up to see us incorporate the video into our lesson. It also gave him a space to share his perspective and experience at his comfort level. This is an example of the type of insight and resources that EL teachers can bring to a co-teaching partnership that can enhance learning for all students.

During another co-teaching partnership in an English 9 class, we were reading *Lord of the Flies*. We were discussing the importance of symbols within the book and asked the class what they thought the conch symbolizes. I wanted to make sure students understood what a conch is. I encouraged our EL students to think of what the cognate of conch is. A student responded, "It's concha, a Mexican bread that I love to eat." Although concha is the correct cognate, the student applied it to the context he was most familiar with, a Mexican pastry. Bringing a cultural lens allowed me to understand where the student was coming from and encouraged him to think of other definitions of a conch that would fit the context of *Lord of the Flies*. Although the student initially did not utilize the correct context for a conch in Spanish, his experience was still validated. It was essential to understand where his thought process was and how to help him make the necessary connections to build his understanding of symbolism in a text.

When co-planning in any class, I like to think critically about the language students need to access the content. I look at where there are opportunities to bridge students' native language with English to allow students to make connections that will help them develop their language skills. Emphasizing cognates is an excellent way to tap into the language assets that students bring to the classroom.

I recall co-planning during an English unit where there were quite a few words that I knew our EL students were not familiar with, yet these were critical for understanding the text. Several of the words were cognates. I suggested to the teacher that we create a word wall where we not only defined words, but also included cognates as much as possible. Students commented on how helpful it was for them to be able to use Spanish to make the meaning of the words they were learning in English. At the end of the unit, we saw an improvement in the way students were able to use the vocabulary in a correct and meaningful context. EL teachers are able to share specific strategies and scaffolds that would support student learning and make the content accessible.

Although I know I have been able to offer a lot of insight to my co-teachers, they have also provided me with a lot of insight into their content area that has allowed me to be a more effective EL teacher. In all of the schools where I have been an EL teacher, a class period is used as a "resource" hour where students receive support on homework for their content classes. Having the opportunity to co-teach and learn from the expertise of content teachers has prepared me to incorporate that knowledge into the resource classes with confidence.

In my experience, with an effective co-teaching partnership, co-teaching has been one of the most transformational methods to improve instruction for ELs. I will never forget one of my most successful co-teaching partnerships. I was co-teaching an Algebra class, and after the first week of school, a student stopped me and asked, "Mrs. Monterrey, who is the real teacher in this class? One day I think it's Mrs. Senger, but then I think it's you. I'm used to seeing one teacher in the back of the room while the other one teaches. You are both doing equal teaching!" Even students can tell the difference when there is a real shared responsibility in the classroom.

## The Importance of Collaborating With Counselors

In addition to collaborating with content teachers, it is imperative for EL teachers to collaborate with school counselors. Counselors play a pivotal role in serving ELs, yet many school counselors are not bilingual and may need assistance with communicating with students and families for the scheduling process or other academic needs. ELs come to our districts from many different countries and with varying academic and language skills. When a new EL student enrolls in a district, it is imperative to have clear protocols on how transcripts will be transcribed and how proper course placement will be determined.

In the first district I taught at, the Student Services department used an outside company to transcribe credits. In my current district, I work with the counselors to review the students' transcript and transcribe the credits. It is beneficial for the counselor and me to do this process collaboratively because we can ensure that the credits are being transcribed according to what would be equivalent to our district's graduation requirements. Once the transcript has been transcribed, I once again collaborate with the student's counselor to develop a schedule for the student. It is extremely important that there will be strong collaboration between EL teachers and counselors for proper course placement and to ensure that students are on the path toward meeting all of their graduation requirements.

I'll never forget working with Monica, who moved from Venezuela her senior year. My heart went out to her for having to leave her country and start a new life in a place where she knew very little English, didn't know many people, and had to adapt to an entirely new school system and culture. She was nervous about not meeting all of our graduation requirements and scared about not having enough English skills to go on to college. I assured her I would give her the necessary support to accomplish her goal of graduating from high school. When we received her transcript, I met with Monica and her counselor to work as a team to review her transcript and ensure that her credits were transcribed appropriately. Through conversations with Monica about her coursework in Venezuela, and a careful analysis of her transcript we were able to ensure that she was in the appropriate classes with the appropriate support for her to graduate with her graduating class.

Recently, I received a message from Monica where she wrote, "I really appreciate everything you did for me and my family! You were a big part of my journey, and I cannot thank you enough for helping me through high school. It was a tough time for me as I was coming from Venezuela with the little English I knew back then so you definitely helped me get through that hard time. Thank you." The work we do to collaborate to ensure the success of students is paramount. Sometimes, we may not realize the impact of our work, but I know students see it and value it.

## Concluding Thoughts

Providing quality programming for ELs takes getting to know the student population and community well. There is not a one size fits all approach when designing a program for ELs. Each school may have its unique needs and requires careful evaluation to determine the best approach to address the needs of the student population. Quite often, EL teachers wear many hats. Although the work can feel exhausting, it is also incredibly gratifying. The population of ELs is here to stay and putting the responsibility to ensure their success solely on the EL teachers is no longer acceptable. English Learners are a part of our schools and communities; therefore, building staff capacity to excel in addressing English Learners' needs is critical to ELs success.

## Reflection Questions

1. What do you do to create a welcoming environment for English Learners in your classroom?
2. What do you do to provide English Learners the appropriate scaffolds needed to be successful in your classroom?
3. Is there someone in your school who you can reach out to and collaborate with to discuss ways to improve instruction for English Learners?
4. Does your school use Individualized Language Plans? If not, is this something that would be helpful for you to implement in your school?
5. What types of professional development do you think is needed at your school to improve the quality of education for English Learners?
6. What is a takeaway from this chapter that you can implement in your classroom or school?

## References

Beninghof, A., & Leensvaart, M. (2016). Co-teaching to support ELLs. *Educational Leadership, 73*(5), 70–73.

Flores, B. B., Claeys, L., Gist, C. D., Clark, E. R., & Villarreal, A. (2015). Culturally efficacious mathematics and science teacher preparation for working with English learners. *Teacher Education Quarterly*, 42(4), 3–31.

Greenberg, J. B., & Vélez-Ibáñez, C. G. (1992). Formation and transformation of funds of knowledge among U.S.-Mexican households. *Anthropology & Education Quarterly*, 23(4), 313–335. doi: https://doi.org/10.1525/aeq.1992.23.4.05x1582v.

Hadjioannou, X., Hutchinson, M. C., & Hockman, M. (2016). Addressing the needs of 21st-century teachers working with culturally and linguistically diverse learners. *CATESOL Journal*, 28(2), 1–29.

Pearson, P. D., & Gallagher, M. C. (1983). The instruction of reading comprehension. *Contemporary Educational Psychology*, 8, 317–344.

Sugarman, J. (2018). *A Matter of Design: English Learner Program Models in K-12 Education*. 20.

# 9

# Welcoming and Inspiring Students

In a time when it feels like there is so much division in our nation, it is more important than ever to build positive relationships with students to create an inclusive school climate. If students do not feel welcome, valued or respected, it is difficult to have a positive learning environment in which students can learn.

My family immigrated to the United States when I was one year old from El Salvador, a country that was torn by a civil war. Being Latina and going through the U.S. public educational system in three different states, allowed me to experience firsthand how issues of equity impact students across all contexts and the importance of building relationships with students so that they feel welcome. It was 1981 when my family and I arrived in Hempstead, New York, our new home. In 1990, we moved to Waukegan, Illinois, a suburb of Chicago, and in 1994, we moved to Lake Geneva, Wisconsin, a small touristy town.

With our family's moves, I went from attending a school that was predominantly students of color, to a school with mostly White and Latinx students to a high school that was predominantly white. It was when I attended a mostly white high school that I often felt like an outsider. It was the first time I experienced having racial slurs hurled at my Latinx peers and me. Going through an educational system where I did not always feel my

DOI: 10.4324/9781003177333-13

culture was valued makes creating a welcoming environment where all students feel safe and valued and having a culturally relevant classroom my top priorities.

## Creating a Welcoming Class Environment

How can educators create a welcoming classroom environment? It's the little things! I like to start by greeting students by name and with a smile at the door. I recall about eight years ago, my principal encouraged all staff members to be out in the halls during the passing period and to greet students as they walked into our classroom. My first thought was, "I don't have much time to transition from one class to the next!"

I quickly discovered it was possible. What I also discovered is that students enjoyed being greeted at the door. Frequently, students will stop and want to chat about various happenings in their day. Now, greeting students at the door before each class is something I look forward to because it is a simple step, I can take to set a positive tone as students walk into my room. In the communication that I send out to teachers at the beginning of the year to share our EL department's demographics, I end by stating, "Remember, a smile is universal!" Even if you cannot communicate well with an EL student, they will sense how you make them feel. Teachers have a lot of control over the classroom environment and how students feel when they walk through the door.

Another simple step we can take to make students feel welcome and safe is to have positive messages in our classrooms. Through the years, I have had the opportunity to work with many students who are DREAMers. In conversations with these students, they have often expressed having feelings of fear and anxiety. Even the most minor steps we take as a school community to make students feel welcome and safe can go a long way.

A few years ago, I had the opportunity to offer my colleagues a professional development session on immigration policies and their impact on students. The professional development session took place in August, right before school started. I ended the session by sharing with staff a "DREAMERs Welcome" poster and a "This School Welcomes You" poster created by Learning for Justice. I printed about 35 copies of the poster and had them available for staff to take as they left the session. To my surprise, all 35 posters were taken, and I received emails from teachers asking me for more posters. The posters were placed on doors for students to see as they walked into classrooms.

When school started, one of the DREAMer students entered my classroom with excitement and said, "Mrs. Monterrey, have you seen all the DREAMers Welcome posters all over the school?!" Other students also commented on the posters. Their words were confirmation that even an action that may be viewed as so simple can go a long way. If posters that state that ALL students are welcomed are displayed, those words need to be put into action.

Once students walk through the doors, teachers must create a sense of community where EVERY student feels they belong. Especially at the high school level, it is easy to fall into thinking that there is too much content to cover and that there is not enough time to spend on icebreakers or community-building activities, but taking the time to build community can have a significant impact on engaging ELs and setting them up for success in our class. As part of community building, learning how to pronounce each students' name is essential. Taking the time to learn how to pronounce names correctly demonstrates inclusion and value in who each student is as an individual.

Making each individual feel they belong contributes significantly to students wanting to be in school. Especially for ELs, it is imperative to have a classroom or space where they feel they can call it their "home" in school. When students walk into my room, I want it to be a place in which they want to be. About six years ago, our school organized a school-wide service-learning day. I asked students how they felt about our classroom and any changes they would like to make to make it feel more welcoming. We agreed that it would be neat to paint the room and add decor to make it more inviting. We spoke with our principal, and she approved for us to have a group of students paint and redesign our classroom as part of our service-learning day.

Students selected a color scheme, and I contacted our local Sherwin Williams to ask if they would be willing to donate paint for our project. Not only did Sherwin Williams donate paint, but they donated paintbrushes and other supplies. In my experience, community businesses are willing and eager to help; it is a matter of asking. With students, we created a space that students enjoy being in and is their go-to place at school. We created a bulletin board where we displayed pictures of students participating in sports, extracurriculars or other school activities. Our goal is to celebrate all the positive things students are doing. Many students who are not in the EL department and walk by our room regularly comment on how cool our room is and how they wish they had a class in that classroom.

When we uplift students and highlight student assets, it creates a positive energy that inspires and motivates students to do well and be engaged in school. All of these small components contribute to creating a safe and welcoming environment.

## Utilizing Students' Funds of Knowledge

Once a welcoming and safe environment has been established, teachers can draw upon the knowledge students already possess and build from there. Students walk into our classrooms with a variety of life experiences. ELs must not be viewed from a deficit mindset but rather an asset-based mindset where educators tap into students' funds of knowledge (Colombo et al., 2019). By building off of students' funds of knowledge, we are valuing and empowering them. When educators shift to viewing ELs from an asset-based mindset, the benefits are reciprocal. Students feel validated and teachers can learn much from their EL students' lived experiences, which contributes to relationship building.

By learning about students' life experiences, teachers can also be purposeful in lesson planning by seeking opportunities to incorporate students' interests within the curriculum. I recall working with a group of students who often talked about not wanting to read. Whenever we went to the library to choose books for our independent reading time, this particular group of students always complained and expressed how much they disliked reading.

I thought about the many assets each student possessed and used what I knew about them to help them select books that would engage them. For example, I knew one of the students loved to play soccer. We found several books that dealt with soccer that caught his interest. He then expressed excitement about reading the book he chose instead of the previous week when he was telling his classmates he never reads because there are no books that interest him.

Another example of incorporating students' interests into the curriculum happens to be one of my favorite assignments from one of my English classes. After reading several of the vignettes in Sandra Cisneros' book House on Mango Street, students chose various topics and wrote vignettes about their own lives. The final product was a small book of vignettes which is one of my favorite projects to read. I learned so much about students while they practiced their writing skills in an engaging manner.

## Providing Students With Role Models

As educators, we get to spend nine months out of the year with our students. Although the exact number may vary from state to state, students are in school for roughly 180 days a year. Within those 180 days, educators have ample time to inspire students and impact their lives. One of the most impactful ways to inspire ELs is to provide them with role models. ELs must know that they are not alone; others have had similar experiences as them and have achieved success.

Quite often there are community members who have powerful stories. Reaching out to community members to share their stories with students has excellent potential for inspiring and motivating students. Hearing inspirational stories from community members who can serve as role models gives students hope and helps them to see what is possible. I have had guest speakers who are people of color working in various fields, from social workers, financial advisors to even admission counselors at our local universities.

A guest speaker who is always a student favorite is my buddy from college, Eric. Eric is a financial advisor who students seem intrigued by because of his compelling story and authenticity. Eric shares with students that he was the first in his family to graduate from college. He shares the stark differences in experiences from some of his relatives who have had to do jail time to his experience as a successful financial advisor making over six figures. One of the most essential life lessons that Eric shares with students is learning how to code-switch. He talks about loving hip-hop, wearing sweatpants, his cap and even earrings. However, you will find him on the job with his suit on, tie nicely done, shining shoes and no earrings. He shares with students the importance of knowing what is appropriate in each setting to experience success. Like Eric, I have been able to bring several other speakers who have shared valuable experiences and life lessons that students have stated have been impactful for them.

I recommend creating a document where you make a list of all the people you know who would be impactful as guest speakers in your class. Include their contact information and be purposeful in your planning to determine the best time to invite them. If you only have a small number of guest speakers in mind, ask colleagues for recommendations, reach out to local non-profit organizations, local universities, or family and friends. You may be surprised at the rich experiences within your local community that can significantly impact students.

A huge advantage technology offers today is the ability to communicate with those who are even hundreds of miles away. An EL teacher I started following on Twitter a few years ago is Emily Frances from North Carolina. Emily has such an inspirational story, and I knew many of my EL students would be able to relate to her experiences. Emily's story is so inspirational that she was even on the Ellen Degeneres show.

I was co-teaching an English class, and while working on a unit about overcoming obstacles, I shared the idea with my co-teacher about highlighting Emily's story. We found a great article about Emily and shared Emily's clip on the Ellen show with the class. I messaged Emily and asked if she would be willing to do a Google Hangout with our class. She graciously agreed. On the day of the Google Hangout, I was filled with joy to see how engaged students were and how impactful it was to have students have a dialogue with Emily.

What was powerful about incorporating Emily's story in our curriculum is that the class was made up of EL students and non-EL students. For many of the non-EL students, it was the first time they heard someone share their immigration story and an EL student's challenges. For the EL students, I could see hope in their eyes as Emily shared her experiences. Much of what Emily shared they were able to relate to, and they had an example of someone who overcame many of the same challenges they faced. Giving students hope and helping them see themselves in stories of success can be transformational!

## Helping Students Prepare for Life After High School

Once students see that they too can have a bright future, educators can inspire students by creating opportunities to learn about post-secondary options. The process of getting to college can be overwhelming for any family; for many ELs it can be daunting. The EL department can play a pivotal role in providing students with the support they need to get to college. Traditionally, there is a lot more focus on discussions about post-secondary options with juniors and seniors, but there is significant value in engaging students in conversations about college and how to prepare for life after high school beginning in their freshman year.

In the beginning of my career, I worked with many students who did not know what the college process was like. Many of them did not know what a cumulative Grade Point Average (GPA) or a transcript was until they got to their junior or senior year. By then, students struggled to improve their GPAs. When I shared critical information with students about college and the many ways doing well in high school could help them, they regularly said, "I wish I would have known this sooner." Hearing students' comments prompted me to begin focusing on providing students opportunities to build their knowledge around post-secondary options and the process to get to college students' freshman year.

I recall having a conversation with a colleague where we both wondered if starting to talk about post-secondary options in freshman year was too early. Would that seem too overwhelming to students? We concluded that if students can be negatively influenced by other factors, such as gangs, drugs, etc., talking about post-secondary options could be what keeps students focused on their futures. It could be what gives some students hope and a reason to strive to do their best. If students know early on what it takes to get to college, they can know how to prepare and be set up for success as opposed to getting to their senior year and wishing they knew the information earlier.

Since EL programs look vastly different depending on the school, EL teachers need to examine their program carefully to determine the best approach to provide students support with post-secondary planning. In my experience, I have been able to provide ELs that much-needed support through a class called VISION (Valuing Individual Student/Success and Increasing Opportunities Now). In VISION students receive support in their content classes and receive instruction on valuable life skills. VISION has been the ideal place to emphasize building students' knowledge about post-secondary options. If you are an EL teacher, I encourage you to examine the EL program model being used and identify an area in which emphasis can be placed on post secondary options. The table below provides a scope and sequence of information around post-secondary options shared with students according to their grade level.

| Grade Level | Post-Secondary Information |
| --- | --- |
| 9th Grade | - Explicitly teach what a high school transcript and a cumulative GPA is and why it is important<br>- Have a panel of college students share their college journey<br>- Set up a college visit<br>- Encourage participation in Pre-College Programs<br>- Explain the difference between an Associate's degree, Bachelor's degree, Master's degree and Ph.D.<br>- Stress the importance of involvement in extracurricular activities and volunteer opportunities |

*(Continued)*

| Grade Level | Post-Secondary Information |
|---|---|
| 10th Grade | - Have students check to see what their cumulative GPA is<br>- Set up college visits including a pane of students from similar backgrounds to share their college journey<br>- Reinforce concepts taught in 9th grade<br>- Continue to encourage participation in Pre-College programs<br>- Explicitly teach about the different options to pay for college<br>- Explain the terms scholarship, financial aid and loan<br>- Stress the importance of involvement in extracurricular activities and volunteer opportunities |
| 11th Grade | - Set up college visits<br>- If possible, have parents also attend the college visits<br>- Explain the financial aid process<br>- Explain the difference between subsidized loans and unsubsidized loans<br>- If possible, set up job shadowing experiences<br>- Take interests surveys to discuss careers of interest |
| 12th Grade | - Begin applying for colleges<br>- Search and apply for scholarships<br>- Set up college visits to the schools students are applying to<br>- Set up a FAFSA Night for families with financial aid advisors from local colleges and universities |

One of the biggest takeaways from my years of teaching is the importance of utilizing the resources available in our communities. Collaborating with local Pre-College programs has been instrumental in motivating students and preparing them with invaluable skills. One of our local universities runs an after-school program within some of the middle and high schools in our district to provide students with academic support. They also include lessons on topics such as how to write a resume, job interview skills, do's and don'ts on a job and much more. Connecting students to Pre-College programs or any other programs provided in the community allows educators and community members to collaboratively be more efficient at providing students a well-rounded support system that can be transformational for a student's trajectory.

One of the best ways to get students excited about college is to take them on college visits. Many Pre-College programs and admissions offices offer college visits that allow students to see what college campuses are like. I have also collaborated with personnel from Multicultural Resources Centers at our local universities to set up student panels during our visits where college students can share with our high school students about their college experiences. For some of the field trips that I have arranged, the universities paid for the cost of bussing and lunch. When funding for bussing is not available through the university, the bussing has been paid for by our school district. Every year students ask me which colleges we will be visiting that particular year. They look forward to having the opportunity to be on a college campus and get an idea of what college life is like.

A couple of years ago, when I was teaching the senior VISION class, I had several students who were interested in one specific university that was about 45 minutes away from our school. That fall, I organized a field trip to that university. When I was working out the details of our visit with the admissions office personnel, they informed me that they had someone on staff who was a native Spanish speaker and could do any portion of our visit in Spanish if needed. I saw it as a prime opportunity to invite parents to join us on the trip.

It was wonderful to see the students and parents learning together about the various programs the university offers. For the majority of the parents, it was their first time on a college campus. It was extremely valuable for parents to be able to see the campus for themselves and get their questions answered in their native language. I particularly enjoyed seeing their reaction to the dorms. Having parents on the college visit with us made the experience so much more meaningful for our students because they were getting the same information together which led to great discussions about how to determine if a college or university is the right fit.

Recently, I had a student who went on that field trip with her parents and contacted me to tell me that she was graduating with her Bachelor's degree. She wanted to get my advice about whether she should pursue her master's degree right away or find a job first. She thanked me for setting up that field trip and all the guidance and support she received from our department during her high school years.

When we think of post-secondary options for students, we must also discuss options in trade areas and jobs for students who would like to enter the workforce immediately after graduation. As much as we may want all students to go to college right away, the reality is that every student's circumstance is different. Discussing with students all the options available to them will help them be better prepared as they enter a new stage in their life.

For some students, it is scary to think about life after high school. Understandably, many students do not know what career path they would like to follow. An approach I have used with students who want to explore career options is setting up job shadow experiences. I ask students what their top three careers would be and do my best to arrange a day for that student to shadow someone who is in that career field. I try my best to set up the job shadow experience on a day that we do not have school, so as not to interfere with their academics. Students have expressed job shadowing being one of the most valuable experiences to help them determine if a career is right for them.

One of my students was interested in becoming a veterinarian. I called a veterinary clinic in town, introduced myself, and explained my desire to set up a job shadowing experience for a student. After speaking to one of the veterinarians, the job show experience was approved. My student, Gabi, was able to spend an entire day shadowing a vet and asking questions about the process of becoming a veterinarian. For me, the most exciting part is the discussion I have with students after their job shadow experience. Gabi shared with me that after learning more about becoming a veterinarian and the responsibilities of a vet, she would rather become a veterinarian technician. She explained that the veterinarian technician interacts more with animals than the vet. Gabi investigated the process of becoming a veterinarian technician and decided that is the career she would like to pursue instead. I was happy that Gabi had such a valuable experience that allowed her to get a better idea of what career she was interested in.

Helping students prepare for life after high school is an excellent way to increase motivation and student engagement. By helping students make the connection between why it is important to do well in high school and how doing well can lead to them being better prepared as they graduate and enter a new stage in life, school becomes more relevant to them. When school becomes relevant, it helps motivate students to do their best. As educators, we play an instrumental role in supporting students as they explore post-secondary options and prepare for their futures.

## Working With DREAMers

One of the most challenging aspects of working with ELs is when students are DREAMers. DREAMers are students who were brought to this country at a young age and are undocumented. In 2012, President Obama implemented the Deferred Action for Childhood Arrival (DACA), which provided a two-year relief from deportation to undocumented individuals who met several key criteria (U.S. Citizenship and Immigration Services, 2014). In President Obama's remarks about DACA (2012) he stated, "These are young people who study in our schools, they play in our neighborhoods, they're friends with our kids, they pledge allegiance to our flag. They are Americans in their heart, in their minds, in every single way but one: on paper. They were brought to this country by their parents—sometimes even as infants—and often have no idea that they're undocumented until they apply for a job or a driver's license, or a college scholarship."

The way President Obama described DREAMers is my experience with DREAMers. I have worked with several students who did not find out about their immigration status until they wanted to get their driver's license and their parents had to explain to them why that was not possible. DREAMers have a special place in my heart because, for these students, there is an added level of stress and anxiety when thinking about their futures.

Working with DREAMers requires extra sensitivity because some students are open about their immigration status while others prefer to keep that information private. The landmark case Plyer vs. Doe prohibits public schools from inquiring about a student's immigration status. While Plyer vs. Doe ensures undocumented students receive the K-12 public education they deserve, there is no mandated regulation once students graduate from high school.

When I first started teaching in 2002, DACA did not exist. At that time, it was particularly challenging to encourage undocumented students to explore post-secondary options because there were not many options available to them in Wisconsin. Students were required to provide a social security number when applying to any public college or university in the state.

When DACA was implemented in 2012, it gave DREAMers hope, and it opened up new opportunities. Although this was a step in the right direction, it still had its challenges in Wisconsin and several other states. Wisconsin is considered a lockout state, which means that although DACA students could now apply to public colleges and universities, they would have to pay out-of-state tuition if accepted. For many students, thinking of the financial burden of paying out-of-state tuition would discourage them from continuing their post-secondary education.

I have been fortunate to work with some outstanding and dedicated students who did not let that deter them. We worked together to look for scholarships that would cover most of their education costs. One scholarship that I highly recommend for DACA students is The Opportunity Scholarship sponsored by TheDream.US. This scholarship is designed for DACA students from lockout states, and it covers full tuition and board to four specific universities. The name of The Opportunity Scholarship is fitting because it opens up a window of opportunities for students that would not be possible without this scholarship.

I have had three students be awarded the Opportunity Scholarship, and they are on their way to completing their degrees at Eastern Connecticut University. Working with DREAMers is a perfect example of why it is imperative for EL teachers to build trusting relationships with students. DREAMers require a unique level of support, and they will only reveal that they are a DREAMer if they have educators they can trust. Once students reveal that they are a DREAMer, it is vital to keep them motivated and support them in their journey as they seek to determine the best post-secondary options available to them.

## The Importance of Building Relationships

Oftentimes we think equipping teachers with strategies is the solution for ELs to experience academic success in content classes; however, that is only one component. One of the most critical components is building relationships with students. Consequently, I emphasize with staff that giving a smile and creating a welcoming environment is paramount. I also emphasize the importance of believing in our students.

I often think of Rita Pierson's TED Talk "Every Kid Needs a Champion" (2013). I share her belief in the importance of human connection. Students will thrive when teachers spend the time to build relationships with them. It is vital that we get to know our students and be champions for them.

When I think of building staff capacity to work with ELs and the pivotal role that relationship building plays, I often question, "How do I foster the desire for staff to focus on relationship building?" I have concluded that the best approach I can take is to model it. I have witnessed how building relationships with students can be transformational. Modeling to my colleagues how simple steps, such as greeting students at the door, asking students about their weekend, talking to them about their interests, are doable steps that can be instrumental in relationship building.

Students know when someone genuinely cares about their success. I have seen students demonstrate tremendous growth when working with educators whom they know believe in them. When students know that we believe in them, they feel valued, which in turn motivates them to learn to their full potential.

My philosophy has always been that I want to treat every student in the same manner that I would want my own children to be treated. We know that every student is unique and that students walk into our schools from many different backgrounds and walks of life. No matter what level any student is at or where they are coming from, THEY CAN LEARN. As educators, we need to believe in every student even when they do not believe in themselves.

In my early teaching career, I worked with a student, Carlos, whom I knew had such great potential. Unfortunately, he began socializing with a group of students involved in gang activity, and they began to negatively impact Carlos. His grades began to decline, and he began skipping some classes. As soon as I noticed these changes, I spoke with the student about it and encouraged him to start making wiser decisions and focus on school. A couple of weeks went by, and the same pattern continued. I spoke with the student again and told him I would be contacting his parents to make them aware of the situation. I explained that I was going to call home because I cared about his education and his future and that his parents did too.

I called his parents that same night. They thanked me for taking the time to call and making them aware of what was happening. The next day at school, Carlos did not speak to me. Even when I greeted him, he just looked at me and kept walking. Carlos did not speak to me for about two weeks.

Suddenly, one day, he started talking to me again. He apologized for not wanting to talk to me for two weeks and explained that he was upset that I called his parents. I explained to him that from the perspective of a teenager, I understood why he was upset, but I was an adult who cared about his future and knew that the right thing to do was to contact his parents so that we could work as a team to ensure his success. I let him know that I believed he had great potential and could have a bright future if he made wise decisions and focused on his education.

Carlos made a turnaround and improved his grades and attendance. Months went by when suddenly one of his teachers stopped and said, "I have to share with you that I have Carlos in one of my classes. We are journaling, and the other day he wrote about you. He stated that you saved his life." That is a moment I'll never forget because it was an affirmation of the impact educators can have on students when building relationships with students and families. I still keep in contact with Carlos today, and I am proud of the man he has become.

When we think of ELs, we often think of the academic challenges they face, but it is vital to look at the whole child and seek opportunities for ELs to also get involved in the school through extracurricular activities. Studies have shown that students who are involved in extracurricular activities are more engaged in school. When ELs join sports and clubs, it helps them develop a stronger sense of belonging in the school community.

About 12 years ago, I observed a significant need to focus on empowering the girls in the EL department. It is no secret that the teenage years are a critical stage in life in which young people need a great deal of guidance and support. I noticed that many girls in my school were dealing with low self-esteem, depression and, frankly, a lot of drama. But the real wake-up call for me came when four students in the EL department at my school became pregnant. I realized that the girls at our school needed a safe space to discuss issues they were facing without judgment.

With this in mind, I started a group the next school year called Girl Talk, with a mission to inspire high school girls to have a voice, be decision-makers, develop problem-solving skills, and create visionary change in their schools and communities. When I first started Girl Talk, it was designed for students in the EL program, with preventing teen pregnancy being a major focus. Since then, the group has evolved. Although we still discuss the importance of preventing teen pregnancy, I strive to give students a voice and have them guide the topics discussed in our meetings. Students have asked to discuss other topics, such as overcoming feelings of depression, distinguishing between healthy and unhealthy relationships, and developing leadership skills.

The group itself has also grown, and the club is open to anyone in the school. Once attended by ten students, our weekly meetings are now attended by about 25–30 students each year. The past few years, it has been wonderful to see how the students—the majority of whom are students of color and English Learners—have blossomed. Girl Talk is one of the most active clubs in our school, and participating students, who span all grade levels, are viewed as leaders because of activities that they organize for the whole student body.

I often get asked for suggestions on how someone would start a club like this at their school and have developed a list of recommendations:

First, establish ground rules. In order for students to feel comfortable, it is essential to establish ground rules for meetings, with the most important rule being "What is said here stays here."

Since we focus so much on the importance of girls empowering each other, it helps set the tone for a safe, trusting environment in which everyone is comfortable to share. Students are also informed that if they share certain information, such as if they are being harmed or having suicidal thoughts, I am obligated as their teacher to report it and get them help.

Second, let students take the lead. I try to give girls in the group as many opportunities as possible to develop leadership skills so that they recognize they have something to contribute to our school—and in life. Students lead and run every Girl Talk meeting. When they have ideas about things they would like to see go differently at our school, I let them schedule meetings with the principal and propose their ideas.

They also share ideas about what projects they would like Girl Talk to focus on or topics for our group to discuss. These have ranged from the signs of an unhealthy versus healthy relationship, how to speak up for yourself, how to deal with abuse and college admissions. For particular topics, some Girl Talk members have launched their own outreach and advocacy at our school.

Third, build community connections. I've made it a point to connect the girls to the community as much as possible. We have great local leaders doing amazing work, and the more role models we can provide students with, the more likely students are able to see themselves in leadership roles in the future. We have community leaders—many of whom are women of color—come in and speak with our students, or we go to their sites to learn about the services they offer. Every year, someone from the Women's Center, a local organization that provides safety, shelter and support to empower all impacted by abuse and violence, comes and speaks with our group, and we visit the center and take a tour.

Fourth, get outside of school. I have students volunteer so that they can see themselves as leaders in the community. Whenever local elementary schools need volunteers for events, Girl Talk is one of the first groups they contact. We have done face painting, served food and run games at various events. We have also done some outreach serving homeless people and even started our own scholarship fund. Often, students don't realize the many skills they have to offer to help others and their community, but through these volunteer experiences, they can develop valuable skills such as empathy and responsibility and learn to appreciate all that they have.

I have been fortunate enough to have some of the Girl Talk members as students in classes that I co-teach. When the COVID-19 pandemic hit and schools had to shut down, our final project for the English 10 class I co-taught was to present a speech titled, "This I Believe." Students were to think about something they believe is essential in life and create and record a speech about it. I had a proud moment when one of our students, a Girl Talk member, focused her speech on the importance of giving back to our communities. She shared that Girl Talk helped her to see how giving back is a simple act of kindness that can make a huge difference in the world. She stated, "Girl Talk made me see that my work as an individual matters and seeing my work make a difference helped me believe in the importance of giving back to my community."

Girl Talk has become such a well-known group in the community that even one of our local news stations came to our school to interview students and aired a segment on the local news about the club. The news coverage can be seen on Youtube at https://www.youtube.com/watch?v=eGwX3G7Z3X0

Through Girl Talk, I have learned that all students are dealing with something. Most teenagers want to talk about the issues and struggles they are facing, but many don't have a safe space in which to do so. For me, Girl Talk has reaffirmed the importance of relationship building and having classrooms where students feel safe in order to maximize their learning. Our alumni regularly contact me to let me know how much they miss Girl Talk and the significant impact it had on their lives after they've left high school. Providing a sisterhood for girls, especially those who are marginalized, can be life-changing.

## Concluding Thoughts

Teachers have the capability to transform students' lives. We have a responsibility to get to know our students well, identify barriers that exist for them and be their advocates, especially those who have many hurdles to overcome. However, we cannot do the critical work of closing opportunity gaps alone. It is the responsibility of ALL educators, administrators and school personnel to work together to address English Learners' needs. We must collaborate to provide them with the best educational experience possible. When English Learners know that we genuinely care about their success and provide them with the support they need to be successful, we will see tremendous student growth. Let's continue to collaborate, advocate and grow together to provide our ELs with the quality education they deserve.

##  Reflection Questions

1. What steps do you take to create a welcoming and safe classroom environment?
2. How do you build relationships with students?
3. If a student was asked how they feel in your classroom, what would they say?
4. How do you incorporate students' funds of knowledge into your classroom?
5. How do you provide students with opportunities for them to see themselves reflected in the curriculum?
6. Are there adults in your community who you can invite into your classroom to serve as role models for students?
7. In what ways do you collaborate with organizations/ resources in your community to motivate and empower students?
8. What is done at your school to support DREAMers?
9. What is the biggest takeaway from this chapter that you can incorporate into your school or practice?

## References

Cafe Music BGM channel. (2013, May 3). *Every kid needs a champion | Rita Pierson*. https://www.youtube.com/watch?v=SFnMTHhKdkw.

Colombo, M., Tigert, J. M., & Leider, C. M. (2019). Positioning teachers, positioning learners: Why we should stop using the term

English learners. *TESOL Journal*, 10(2), N.PAG. https://doi-org.ezp. waldenulibrary.org/10.1002/tesj.432

Remarks by the President on Immigration. (2012). Whitehouse.Gov. https://obamawhitehouse.archives.gov/the-press-office/2012/06/15/remarks-president-immigratio.

U.S. Citizenship and Immigration Services. (2014). *Daca toolkit*. https://www.uscis.gov/sites/default/files/document/guides/DACA-toolkit.pdf.

WIDA. (n.d.). Retrieved June 3, 2021, from https://wida.wisc.edu/.

# Part 4

# Considerations in Teaching Remotely

*By Mandy Manning, Ivonne Orozco Sahi, Leah Juelke and Sarahí Monterrey*

# 10

# Teaching, Engaging, Building Relationships and Creating Community in a Virtual Classroom

## Preparing Students for Remote Learning—Mandy Manning

When the 2019–2020 school year began, our computer applications teacher retired and was not replaced. This posed a problem for the Newcomer Center. Without an intro computer class, we would have to find an alternative course for our newest immigrant and refugee students to attend. While I understood that art or physical education were possible alternatives, I also knew that without foundational skills in the computer applications we used in our school, students would have a hard time transitioning to the sheltered instruction program and mainstream classes. I advocated for a month and finally succeeded in convincing my administration that I could teach the computer applications class.

After gaining emergency certification (I had been a career and technical education teacher several years prior), I started teaching my students the computer skills they would need as they navigated learning in a U.S. high school. My district uses Microsoft 365. We worked through how to use each of the

DOI: 10.4324/9781003177333-15

programs as they related to classes, with an emphasis on the elements of the program used for organization and independent learning, like email and using Teams to turn in assignments. We also practiced basic typing and desktop navigation.

This instruction proved an important piece of their instruction when spring 2020 rolled around, and COVID-19 descended on the world. Suddenly, with almost no notice, students were expected to learn remotely. They were in class one day and learning from home the next. One reason our Newcomer students were able to navigate the transition at all was because we had spent an entire semester learning the computer programs our school district used in classrooms.

Had I known what was ahead, I'd likely have been even more intentional in my instruction. Students still had gaps, but they had a basic understanding of navigating the programs that would keep them learning. This last year proved that students and educators must be prepared to learn remotely. This means first ensuring students have access to technology at home and assessing whether students have access to high-speed Internet, then taking steps to make sure the school and district are focused on making this happen. Second, educators must utilize district computer programs in their classes in meaningful ways, as well as teach students to use those computer programs to become independent learners at home.

An additional and essential piece is figuring out how to maintain those elements of classroom practice that create community and promote relationships while learning remotely. For Newcomers, at least in my district, that means continuing home visits and that personal face-to-face connection (while following safety protocols, of course). This also means personally checking that students have all of the materials they need to successfully access learning when not in the classroom (i.e., materials, tools, technology, access to Internet).

Beyond those basics, it's important to provide content that students access asynchronously. In my district, students were required to participate in synchronous learning. Students followed the regular school schedule, as if face-to-face. While this is good for maintaining a routine, it isn't equitable for every student. We must provide students with content, teacher-made videos, activities and projects they can be self-directed in utilizing and contribute to their sense of community, ability and understanding, extending their learning and supporting their ability to be independent learners. These skills will not only help them when learning remotely, they will help them as they transition into adulthood, as well.

## Advocacy and Teaching in COVID-19 Times—Ivonne Orozco

In the spring of 2020, we were hosting parent-teacher conferences on campus at my high school. It was in a lull of time between appointments that I talked to one of my neighbor teachers about the seemingly far-away and yet coming closer Coronavirus pandemic. Things were bad in Italy and New York, we heard about school districts thinking about shutting down for a few weeks. We speculated, would they shut us down? No, probably not. We only had a few cases in New Mexico at the time. I read about the toilet paper buying panic and I called my wife after school to ask if I needed to go buy some. She said no. That afternoon, Teachers Against Child Detention (TCAD) Albuquerque was hosting the viewing of Refuge(e) a documentary featuring the experiences of two refugees who had been imprisoned in private, for-profit prisons in the United States. We were being hosted in the building belonging to the Albuquerque Teachers Federation (ATF), our local union. As we showed the film, there was much commotion in the hallway. They seemed to be working on something very important. That evening, our New Mexico governor Michelle Lujan Grisham made the announcement to shut down all New Mexico public schools for at least three weeks.

What strikes me the most about this day is how seemingly normal things had been. Hosting families in my classroom, talking with colleagues, hosting our TACD Albuquerque meeting—although we did set the chairs far apart from people and we did not hug each other, as an early precaution to what would become the norm for the next year. The pandemic was an altering event to all of our lives, and for teachers—it was altering in almost every single aspect of the way we build relationships with students, the way we communicate with parents and with students, and of course, the way we deliver content. For me, the hardest part was the relationship part, I felt flattened and in survival mode. We now know that of course the school closure in March did not last only three weeks, it was extended until the end of the school calendar in May. Then, in August we also started the year remotely.

While in March teachers had been regarded as heroes for adjusting rapidly to the changing demands of our districts, by the time August came to start the school year again, parents were tired. There was much criticism as families looked at neighboring states and the way they were preparing to receive students in person. I am grateful that the Albuquerque teacher's union and our governor protected our students, teachers and every one of our families by deciding to keep us remote.

Teaching online was challenging, and it was very difficult to connect with students, particularly once my district let us know we could not require webcams to be on during Google Meets. I struggled to get to know students, I typically memorize names by the end of the first few days of school—I know how important it is to students that you recognize them as they walk into your classroom. But at the beginning of that year, I simply had a roster and a lot of colorful circles in the Google Meet that appear when students have their cameras off. I could not attach names to students even when I asked them to unmute or type in the chat. I made jokes and nobody laughed, which was quite a blow to my performance ego that is typically on pointe at the beginning of the school year.

All of this to say, remote teaching and learning was hard, probably my worst year as a teacher. Yes, building relationships was a challenge which means that students also struggled with that. Building relationships online creates a whole new level of visibility on inquiries, questions are public, stories are amplified and can be recorded or taken out of context. The spontaneity of community was gone in my Google Meet classes. Of course, this leads to challenges for immigrant families, who may not be able to connect with teachers who can be resources. It becomes a challenge for teachers trying to reach out. For me, it was so much harder to identify students who may be struggling academically, socially or legally regarding immigration issues. In a typical school year, after students learn of my story and background, they confide in me and tell me about their family stories, when their mom took her citizenship test or maybe about an uncle who was deported. Sometimes they tell me about their own struggles with immigration documents and the process of their own applications or lack of. I typically know my students because they know me, and they share with me. The online teaching environment stripped us of the private space for teachers to be confidants the way we can be in person.

In April of 2021, after beginning a strong vaccination campaign, the state of New Mexico mandated that all public schools must offer in-person education options for all K-12 students. So, we returned to the building with students still having the option of learning online. Like most teachers around our country, I taught both in person and online simultaneously. This was only for the last six weeks of school and by the time the last week came around I only had one or two students in person while the rest opted to stay home and connect through our Google Meet. But what I loved about those six weeks is that I had many students come in, and you know what happened? They told me about their immigration stories, their travels to neighboring Mexican state Chihuahua, they said they felt at home with me. Because even though they were not unmuting or sharing their stories in the Google Meets, they were listening to mine. So, I am grateful we returned to in-person learning and I got to know them, even for a little bit.

The interesting part about this work, all of it, is that it never stops or ends. The advocacy for all but particularly immigrant students, teaching and continuous building of teacher community, it just never ends. It is work that requires love, heart and patience. For me, it has meant that I need to recommit often and strongly to the work. I get tired, I am tired, and then the work calls again and I need to show up. I invite you, as a fellow educator, to look into your work again and recommit to it today.

# Tips and Tools for Teaching Remotely—By Leah Juelke

## Engaging Students

Even in a virtual environment, it is crucial to greet students right away when they enter the online class. Just as in the classroom, this lets students know you care about them and that you see them. It is even more important to address students when online, so that you can be certain that their technology is working and that they are ready for class. When working with EL students, the teacher needs to take time to address each student individually at the beginning of class.

It is a good idea for teachers to start class with an interactive bell ringer. Teachers could use this time to review the previous day's lesson, while checking for understanding. Some great platforms for bell ringers are: Padlet, Peardeck, Mente, Answergarden and Nearpod.

Other great ways to engage students include inviting guest speakers to class and having students ask them pre-written questions. I call on students randomly to ask a question and they are free to choose any question on the list. Since they don't go in order, students have to pay attention to make sure they don't ask the same question twice.

Edpuzzle is another amazing resource that engages students by letting the teacher insert questions for understanding in the middle of videos. This ensures that when students are doing asynchronous work that involves videos, they are also paying attention and engaged.

For years, in the classroom, I have had my EL students dress up and act out plays, such as Romeo and Juliet with props and costumes as we are reading them. When we finish a play, students then create their own versions, changing the time or place. This type of tactile and visual learning is important for EL students. Since going online, I struggled with how to provide the same interactive experience for my students. One thing that worked, to make sure the students were engaged while reading the play Romeo and Juliet, was to first assign them parts. I would then share my screen, so everyone could see a copy of the script. I made each student find something in their house that represented their character. For example, some students wore hats, necklaces, aprons or wore a blanket as a cape. Students then had to pay attention to the script and jump in with their line when their time came. I also encouraged the students to change their voices to sound the part. My high school EL students had a blast with this and there were many smiles and giggles as they "acted" out Romeo and Juliet on Zoom.

## Expectations

Teachers should still have class expectations for student participation in online classes. It is easy for students to tune out and passively attend classes. Although a student's name is on the screen, that doesn't always mean they are engaged. Setting online rules at the start of each class is important. I have a slide that I share at the beginning of every class period that reminds students to mute their mics, turn on their cameras, be kind and be present.

Giving every student an opportunity to be a part of the discussion or answer questions is the key to an active online classroom. Make it clear that you expect all students to participate.

To help students meet expectations, teachers should choose activities that students complete in real time, such as posing questions on Padlet or Peardeck. Teachers can post the link in the chat box and students are directed to the platform, where they can answer a question that the teacher created. Students can see other student's replies and the teacher can easily gauge student engagement.

## Pulling in Parents (Parent/Family Involvement)

Engaging parents is a key to student success. Since online or distance learning can often confuse students or parents, it is important that the teacher continually communicates with the families.

My EL students are mainly newly arrived refugees and immigrants from over 20 different countries. Many more barriers to communication exist with my families than with others. For the first couple days of distance learning, I spent hours on the phone with an interpreter and parents. Our school uses a paid for program called Voiance to help communicate with non-English speaking families. A teacher is able to dial the number and select a language provided by Voiance and then the phone number of the parent. It essentially functions as a three-way call with interpretation. This system has helped our district stay in contact with EL families, who are not able to communicate in English.

It is also important to offer families opportunities to be involved in the active learning of the student. For a formal assessment of Romeo and Juliet, students made movies with their peers. Since students in quarantine were not able to work together, the project format changed. Students were encouraged to involve their family members to recreate scenes from the play. Students ended up using parents, grandparents, cousins and siblings. It was fun to see the families spending time together while working on the project. Some students worked with their families and utilized a cartoon maker program called Powtoon or they used inanimate objects around their house, such as forks and spoons to play characters from the play. I was thrilled to see my students being so creative.

Another way to engage parents and families is to create projects that require the families to work together. For my Partnership for New Americans class, students were assigned to create a cooking show. Students included their family members cooking with them and explaining the significance of the meal they were cooking. Students also wrote down the recipe and shared them with each other in class. The videos were posted on Youtube and shared on social media with permission.

An app that is very useful for my EL families was Talking Points. This allows teachers to text parents in English and it will automatically translate into their native language. Teachers set up the app online and designate the native language and family's phone number beforehand. This has been a great way to overcome the language barrier that affects so many of our refugee and immigrant families.

## Organizing Your Lessons

Consistency and routine are keys for EL learners. It is important that students can rely on certain routines to happen when they tune into their online class. Students feel confident if they understand tasks to complete at the start of the class and are more likely to be engaged in learning.

In terms of routine, I always have a bell ringer to start class. I like to use Padlet, Nearpod and Peardeck to ask students questions and get quick answers. It is also useful to have a list of activities for the class, so students know what to expect. Having an exit activity, to check for understanding, is a great way to end a lesson.

For bellringers, I like to have themed days, so students have some consistency and know what to expect right away each day.

- Meme Mondays—students create a meme for the projected picture
- Trivia Tuesdays—students respond to trivia question (Zoom polls, google form, Kahoot)
- Wellness Weds—meditation or physical activity—(Go Noodle, Youtube)
- Thankful Thursday—students write about what they are thankful for each Thursday
- Friday Fun—mini Kahoot, funny educational videos, scavenger hunt, show and tell

## Ensuring Equity in Technology Access

To help ensure equity, our school district worked with the local internet provider and was able to get free internet access for our families in need during distance learning. My district also provided all students with a personal learning device. It is important that all students are able to access materials and the internet to help them be successful if distance learning continues.

## Take Care of Yourself (Staying Balanced)

One of the most important things an educator can do when teaching at a distance is to always be open to new ideas, new technology and new ways of teaching.

Teachers should have an exercise routine of their own while teaching online. Due to the setting, teachers often do not move as much while distance teaching. Setting a timer or alarm to encourage movement is incredibly helpful to get your steps. I like to set my smart watch to active mode and it will remind me to move. I also have a treadmill in my home office and often walk while I am in meetings or in between classes.

I make sure that I still do meal planning while teaching from home. I found out quickly that having the kitchen so close was not a good thing for me. I found myself grabbing unhealthy snacks between classes and indulging more than I would normally. I started planning snacks and meals and this helped me eat in a healthier way.

One of the best ways to stay balanced is to take time to reach out to friends and other teachers. I really like using the Marco Polo app to reach out to my teacher friends. I can leave a video message and my friend is able to listen and respond whenever is convenient for her. Talking about your feelings and sharing your thoughts with another teacher who understands has been one of the most beneficial things I have done for my mental health.

## Supporting ELs' Social-Emotional Learning Remotely—By Sarahí Monterrey

As most educators, I will never forget the early weeks of March 2020, where I would watch the daily news to keep up to date with the latest on the spread of COVID-19. As states began to announce school closures, I wondered, "Are we next?" It was the afternoon of Friday, March 13, when the email came in at around 2:30 pm announcing an emergency staff meeting immediately after school. Our staff then learned that our Governor issued all schools in Wisconsin to shift to distance learning effective immediately to reduce the spread of COVID-19.

Our district has a tremendous advantage because we were already a one-to-one district with each student having a district-issued iPad and students being very familiar with online platforms such as Google Classroom and Blackboard. Even though most teachers and students felt comfortable using technology, having to conduct class virtually was an entirely different ballgame.

I quickly discovered that some students enjoyed the virtual environment and thrived, while others who typically excelled in the face-to-face environment all of a sudden struggled and began to disengage. Thankfully, our EL students had a resource class in our EL department called VISION (Valuing Individual Student/Success and Increasing Opportunities Now), where they received support from an EL teacher to support them in their content courses. During distance learning, I found the VISION class to be even more crucial to ensuring that students passed their classes and stayed engaged in school until the end of the school year. I found that regular communication with students, families and teachers was more important than ever.

All year, I was working with a student, Ricardo, who needed a lot of scaffolds and support in English 10. With the shift to distance learning, I knew it was imperative to communicate with Ricardo, his teachers and his mom regularly to make sure he understood what he had to do to be successful in each class. I recall Ricardo not turning in an important speech for English class on time despite having several conversations with him explaining to him what he had to do. I called his mom to explain to her the importance of Ricardo turning in his speech. When I called his mom and explained the expectations to her, she said, "Muchas gracias por llamar y explicarme todo. Yo le voy a quitar el celular hasta que entregue su trabajo. (Thank you for calling me and explaining everything to me. I will take his cell phone away until he gets his assignment turned in.)" Having his cell phone sure was a motivator for Ricardo, and he turned in his speech right away.

Shortly after, I spoke with Ricardo and asked him why he had not turned his speech in on his own and why it took me calling his mom for him to do it. He said, "I really don't like virtual learning. I have a hard time learning this way. I am losing motivation." Similar to Ricardo, I had several students who skipped their virtual classes, were not turning in assignments and expressed losing motivation. It was a reminder that students still needed to feel connected to each other and that supporting their social-emotional well-being was just as critical as supporting them academically.

Two steps I took to support students' mental health were to create a space where students could express if something was on their mind and they needed to have additional support for me and set up times where our class could simply talk to each other. Students had to complete a Google Form for their VISION class where they wrote down their grades for each class and any missing assignments. On that Google Form, I added a few questions to share how they are feeling and if there is anything on their mind. Depending on what students would write, I would follow up with them.

How are you feeling today? *

○ Happy

○ Stressed

○ Anxious

○ Nervous

○ Relaxed

○ Scared

○ Other: _____

Is there something on your mind that you would like to talk about?

Your answer _____

How much do you need help from me? *

○ I don't need help, I understand everything.

○ I only have a few questions on things. Please contact me.

○ I am lost and need a lot of help. Please contact me.

○ Other: _____

**FIGURE 10.1**

We made it through the 2019–2020 school year, and I was anxious for the summer where I could disconnect from so much technology. The summer flew by, and as the 2020–2021 school year approached, there was much uncertainty as to what the format of instruction would be. Our district began the school year using a hybrid model where all students were virtual on Mondays, and half of the study body alternated attending face-to-face from Tuesday to Friday. Although we had a specific model in place, there were still many changes for students and staff with quarantines and eventually moving to distance learning for a couple of weeks.

Through yet another challenging year, one vital component stood out as critical for teachers and students as they did their best to navigate the challenging year: RELATIONSHIPS! I knew I needed to follow up with students and observe closely to see who was becoming disengaged.

One morning, I decided to call a student who I noticed has been absent virtually for a few days. When I asked her if everything was okay, she responded, "Ms. I don't even feel like getting out of bed to brush my teeth in the morning. I am so depressed. I'm tired of having to quarantine and being home. I don't know how to find motivation." I told her I understood how hard things have been, and we discussed steps she can take to feel better. I asked her if it was okay to email her counselor and her teachers to let them know how she was feeling. Shortly after I sent out the email, several teachers responded, thanking me for making them aware of the situation. They reached out to her and came up with plans for her to get caught up in her classes.

## Concluding Thoughts

While the advancements in technology have facilitated the ability for schools to offer distance learning, nothing can replace the human connection. Paying close attention to student engagement and supporting their social-emotional well-being is paramount.

**Reflection Questions**

1. How can you make remote learning more equitable for each student? (Think about the programs and technology students must be able to navigate and their access to tech and services.)

2. What are some new challenges you've faced in advocating for your students during the pandemic?

3. This chapter included tips for engaging EL students remotely. Which might you try with your own students?

4. How can you prioritize social-emotional learning and relationships in a remote setting?

# Closing

## By Mandy Manning

Neroz and Mohamad are brother and sister. They came to the United States in 2016 as refugees from Syria. When they first came to my classroom, both wore hearing aids. I was told they had suddenly become deaf due to the conflict in their home country, when an explosion tore through their apartment building. Our audiology department would soon fit them with AM/FM systems to amplify my voice during instruction. Although I was told this was all they would need to support their learning, I would come to learn support would be far more fluid than our system generally allowed.

We all know what it feels like to be caught in someone else's bureaucracy. This happens to me every time I have a student in my class who I know needs more than English language instruction. Students who need specialized instruction and, more than that, extra effort and planning in ensuring they feel welcome and that they belong. The bureaucracy Neroz and Mohamad had to navigate is a good example.

My school district consisted of five comprehensive high schools, eight middle schools, 35 plus elementary schools and a smattering of specialty schools, and served roughly 31,000 students. There is a lot of bureaucracy in place which needs to be navigated in order to address an individual student's needs— these protocols serve a purpose within the system, but are cumbersome and do not necessarily serve the students within the system. It's easy to imagine how easy it would be for individual students to get lost.

With Neroz and Mohamad, it was soon quite obvious these two students would need much more than an amplification

DOI: 10.4324/9781003177333-16

system in order to be successful in my class, to feel connected with their classmates and to truly feel welcome in our school and community. One month into the school year, neither student could understand me or their peers nor were they producing any language. Mohamad's expression was usually blank, only responding to visual images, but not able to recognize letters or words. Neither student would respond vocally or produce any other gesture of recognition, beyond copying from the board.

Finding the right person to go to in order to help them be successful was difficult. Systems are not only treacherous for the students stuck in them, but also for the teachers trying to navigate within them. I first tried to go straight to the audiology department, whom I'd had yet to hear from, but I soon found that a single teacher, in one classroom, in such a large district, did not have enough clout to reach out directly to audiology.

In the meantime, I was learning not only about Neroz and Mohamad's hearing needs, but also learning from their personalities, while at the same time navigating an entire classroom of students with their own individual needs. Neroz and Mohamad were delightful. Both were friendly and respectful. Neroz was an incredible student, focused and excited to learn, despite the obstacle of being unable to hear. She tried everyday, copying everything from the whiteboard, and using the whiteboard to communicate her understanding. Neroz managed to gain some understanding and literacy in English and if I'd only paid attention to her, I might have realized they needed so much more than we were offering them.

Mohamad, however, clearly struggled. He was not academically focused and gave up easily, often putting his head on his desk after only an hour of class time. He was totally exhausted because of the seemingly insurmountable barrier of being unable to hear. It was Mohamad who spurred me into action.

I reached out directly to the family, first. Every semester, I went on home visits to meet my students' families. These visits were just one piece of how I built relationships with my students. The visits were always informal, just the Paraeducator I work alongside and me, visiting each home and sitting with the families, learning about them, observing and beginning to build a partnership. These visits communicated with my students that I cared about them beyond the four walls of our classroom, that I was interested in their lives and that I wanted to personally meet their families.

That initial visit with Neroz and Mohamad's family allowed me to observe their interactions with their family and to get a glimpse of their interests outside of school. However, after that visit, I knew I needed to learn more. I invited their parents in for a conference with an interpreter in our classroom. Because of my initial visit to their home and the relationship we had begun to build, they felt comfortable in the meeting and I was able to learn a great deal about their family history.

This is when I learned that Neroz and Mohamad had not recently become deaf. They were born deaf, although not completely. Their hearing had diminished over time, but still when they were quite young, impacting their language acquisition. At the home visit I observed the family using gestures to communicate. At the time, I didn't know sign language, so assumed that's what they were using to communicate. At that official meeting at the school, though, I learned that on top of being profoundly deaf, these two students had spotty formal education, especially Mohamad. Both understood some Arabic signs and Neroz had understanding of Arabic language, but Mohamad had even less understanding. Also, many of the signs they were using at home were rudimentary signs they had created as a family in order to communicate with one another.

Simply being willing to ask, to sit down and have a conversation with those most impacted by the system can change the way we humanize the people within our systems and adjust to meet their needs and ensure they feel welcome and that they belong.

Not knowing where to turn I reached out to my supervisor, who assured me audiology would connect with me soon. I waited, but still, nothing happened, and we were now in our second month of school. Whether it was true or not, I felt I was failing these kids as their teacher and the system was failing them, too. Neroz was making some friends, but Mohamad was still so alone. While this story seems like an indictment of several players, including the audiology department, I need to point out that I wasn't the only one caught up in this bureaucracy—we all were. It would just take a bit of pressure and commitment to help all of us become disentangled in order to put these students before this cumbersome system.

In the workroom one day, I ran into the school nurse and I shared with her my frustrations about getting help for Neroz and Mohamad. She took that information and ran with it. By the end of that week, she'd helped me find sign language classes outside of school.

These classes were put on by a local woman who was also deaf. She was incredible and so willing to accommodate the family—even setting up an individual time just for them. I find that if you look, there are always people in the community willing to help.

I was also able to attend these sign language classes with Neroz and Mohamad and their family in order to be a more effective teacher for them and to help them communicate with their peers in class, by bringing this little bit of sign language back to the classroom. From that point on, I incorporated sign language into every language lesson. This helped all of our students in their language acquisition and ensured Neroz and Mohamad could feel connected with their classmates.

The nurse also helped me set up a meeting with deaf education, audiology and a counselor to figure out exactly what Neroz and Mohamad would need. We had an official meeting with their parents and finally began the process of meeting their needs.

At the close of that first year, through the work of this team of advocates, both students had a 504 plan, which included weekly sign language instruction, and some sign language interpretation during class.

However, our job was not yet done. Spring of that first year our district leaders determined we needed counselors at the high schools specifically dedicated to our English Language Learners. This last addition to our team proved invaluable, because that next fall, Neroz had moved into our sheltered English Language Development program, with a couple of mainstream classes, while Mohamad stayed with me in the Newcomer Center. In the first week of school, it was clear we still lacked adequate interpretation and sign language instruction for both students.

The district assumed we would be able to keep Neroz and Mohamad together, but each of their schedules had shifted based on their learning needs. They were in different places in their language development and their academic abilities. Because we now, thankfully, had a dedicated English Language Learner counselor (an adjustment to the system), I immediately contacted her.

She reached out to the students' sign language instructor, and together they determined Neroz and Mohamad would need individual education plans (IEPs). IEPs are usually reserved for students with developmental or learning differences, not for students who are deaf. So, this was where we were really bucking the system. Not only were we pushing against systems around identification for an IEP, we were also pushing against assumptions about English Language Learners.

We worked together, holding each other accountable for each of our individual pieces. This usually meant a text to my supervisor who helped audiology accountable and a report to the counselors or Deaf Ed. Teacher who held the school psychologist and speech pathologist account.

I handled the IEP paperwork specifically related to English Language Learners. The counselor took care of working directly with the school psychologist and figuring out how to navigate the IEP process. And audiology, the Deaf Ed. instructor and the school nurse worked on specifying the needs of each student and outlining what would need to be included in their IEPs.

By the close of the third semester in our program, because of the commitment of the entire team of advocates, both Neroz and Mohamad had individual sign language instruction twice a week. They each had a dedicated interpreter who attended classes with them. They also continued as a family to take sign language classes out in the community. Their IEPs were in place and both had started speech pathology, because they were beginning, especially Neroz, to hear and make sense of sounds because of their cochlear implants.

When Neroz and Mohamad both left my class, while still having the support of the English Language Development department, they were branching out and taking more mainstream classes with their US born peers. Mohamad played lunch basketball with his friends, and both were becoming fluent in American Sign Language.

I am honored to say that both Neroz and Mohamad are high school graduates. Mohamad is working and Neroz is on her way to college. They are both successful and navigating a community in which they know they belong and feel welcome. None of this would have been possible without a team of school staff coming together to advocate for these two students within this massive system and putting their needs above that system. It is only in this way we are able to create environments in which each of our students is seen, heard, celebrated and welcomed into our schools and our communities.

We do this by, first, **bringing culture into our curriculum** and across our classrooms. Language is the geography of the nations and the cultures of the people who speak it. It is the connection between idea and action. It is what connects us to place and people. Students need to know how learning English will impact them and how it is relevant to their lives, while at the same time honoring the language(s) they already speak and value of maintaining those languages. They must also have the opportunity to use language to share the culture, experiences and ideas they have brought with them in their journey to the U.S.

Leah brings in speakers from the cultures represented by her students. Sarahí brings families into the school. Ivonne helps her students explore their own cultures and heritage. I connect the language we are learning in our classroom with students' experiences in their home countries. We all ensure our classroom environment reflects the cultures of the students within our classes through the images on the walls, the books in our bookshelves and the topics we use in our instruction. How do you bring culture into your classroom?

Next, we must **connect students across classrooms, schools and districts**. Give students the opportunity to use language in a variety of contexts and for a variety of purposes outside of the curriculum and the classroom. One way is through service learning. Sometimes students have to go away to come back home. We must help students seek opportunities that will help them experience the differences they have from others, while recognizing their similarities, too.

Leah helps her students share their stories with a wide audience. Sarahí connects her students with opportunities in the community to help students build their leadership skills. Ivonne encourages her students to explore their identity while connecting with language. I connect my class of students with other classes in the building to build relationships outside of the English Language Development program. We must ensure we are not isolating our students, but rather opening their world to their peers and vice versa. How do you connect students across classrooms, schools and districts?

Next, people are socialized to be ethnocentric, especially in the United States. As language instructors, we have an opportunity to **decentralize ourselves**, to recognize that the U.S. and our culture is not the center of our planet, but rather, one square in a giant quilt, each one just as important as all of the others. We do this through, not only exploring the mechanics of language, but exploring the cultures of the people who speak it.

Leah created a class at the local university for K-12 educators based on her students' stories and strategies for working with EL student Sarahí offers professional development to colleagues on immigration and best practices in servicing English Learners by considering the whole child. Ivonne worked with administration to create a class for heritage language learners to ensure their needs were being met. I work with my colleagues in the English Language Department to share information about the cultures of our students with school staff. We must work to ensure that our schools celebrate and honor the cultures of every student within them. That means learning about cultures and bringing those voices into our classrooms and our lessons. How do you personally work to decentralize yourself and help your colleagues do the same?

We must also **help our students connect across the globe**. Reality is relative. Our lens is made through our experiences. We must give young people an opportunity to explore beyond their borders and not only national borders, but borders between classrooms, towns and cities, and borders between communities.

We can use technology to connect our students with students in another part of the world. We can expose our students to the different ways English is used. The different accents and cultures who speak it.

Leah collaborates with classrooms around the world and organizes Flipgrid and Zoom pen pal experiences to her students. She also encourages her students to explore the United Nations Sustainable Development Goals through projects and school-wide contests, as well as having her students participate in projects run by teachers in Greece, Kenya and many other countries. Because many of Sarahí's students have not lived in the U.S. for too long, much of what is in their community is new to them. Sarahí focuses on helping students see how they can help make a difference in the world through community service. Sarahí has arranged countless volunteer experiences for students that allow them to gain a deeper understanding of their community and our world. Ivonne connects her students to the cultures and diversity of Spanish-speaking cultures and countries by making sure students are thinking about current events critically and are ready to communicate not only touristically but also with cultural knowledge. Because my students are so new to the U.S. we stay close to home. However, students in my classroom come from across the globe, so I ensure they learn from one another's cultures and experiences. Just as it is important for us to decentralize ourselves, we must also help students to do the same in order for them to be open to different ways of being, thinking and doing. How can you connect your students with others across the globe?

Additionally, for English Learners living in an English-speaking country, we must **help them be proud of where they come** from and help them celebrate their roots, the cultures and their languages. Help them connect with their English-speaking peers, not to exploit their stories of their journey to where they are now, but to share their cultures, to build connections, to humanize them and their peers, and to bring relevance to the language they are learning.

Leah teaches empathy and engages her students in projects that showcase and celebrate their authentic selves, while also empowering them to share their stories and advocate for their beliefs within the school, community and beyond. Sarahí has been a strong advocate for expanding Dual Language Programs where students can be proud of their heritage and being bilingual. She co-taught the first Dual Language Spanish IV class at one of her schools. Ivonne had her Spanish heritage-language learner students reflect on their journey speaking Spanish by writing personal narratives. Because I teach Newcomers, I incorporate elements of students' experiences that focus on their most positive memories from their homes before coming to the U.S., like their favorite place or their school and how it differs from school in the U.S. Then we share these memories in a celebratory way. It is important for students to bring their cultures and previous homes with them. We do not want students to assimilate to life in the U.S. We want them to honor their cultures and heritage and bring those gifts with them. We also want their U.S.-born peers to appreciate those cultures and heritage, as well. How do you help students in your school community celebrate, honor and have pride in their cultures and history?

We also have to remember what it's like to walk in a young person's shoes. We must work to **know the students who are in front of you**. Learn their cultures and their experiences. Learn what they need and what they already know. Look for the talents they bring with them. View students, not through perceived gaps or deficits, but rather through their assets. Build from what they have brought with them. Only then can we create relevant and engaging instruction. Rethink what you've always done and adjust to a rapidly changing world. Be flexible. Open the world for your students through experiences. Create opportunities for young people to connect and give them hope.

Leah always starts the year with relay races and team building activities to help her students get to know each other and encourage a collaborative environment. Sarahí starts the school year with an icebreaker that she has adapted and calls "Going on a Train Ride." During the activity, students sit in a circle with one student in the middle. The student in the middle responds to sentence frames that Sarahí provides that elicit students to share about their likes and interests. Students who also share the likes and interests stated have to find a new chair. This musical chair style game allows Sarahí to learn about the assets of her students, and she uses that information to build connections with them throughout the school year. Ivonne makes sure she can pronounce each student's name correctly, always honors preferred names and pronouns and has students practice pronouncing her own name, and explaining why it's so important we get to know each other from the very basics. I start the school year, not with an assessment of my students' academic abilities, but with their interests and talents, through "I am" posters and "getting to know you" activities. By first focusing on who students are outside of the classroom, it's much easier to see the whole child and to then create lessons and activities that will honor those gifts students bring with them. How do your students' assets, gifts and talents each new school year?

Finally, we must **take nothing for granted or make assumptions**. There is so much that we assume students already know how to do when they enter our schools. With English Learners, we can't do this. Navigating the systems within a school in the U.S. can be confusing and become a barrier for English Learners. Things like graduation requirements, understanding how to join a sports team or other extracurricular activities need to be fully explained and modeled. There are other less obvious systems, as well, like navigating the cafeteria and following a bell schedule that need to be expressly taught. We must take nothing for granted.

Leah helps her students understand the community around them and build relationships with peers through her Partnership for New Americans, which is offered to new EL students and students born in the U.S. Students learn about the school system, study skills, traditions, social skills and community resources, while working in a mentor/mentee relationship. Sarahí not only builds students' knowledge on how to navigate our school system through her VISION (Valuing Individual Student/Success and Increasing Opportunities Now) class but also does so with families through the bilingual parent group. Ivonne keeps in mind her own experiences as a new immigrant in middle school and how confusing and overwhelming everything was, for this reason she makes sure students know she is a resource they can come to. Because I teach Newcomers, beginning on the first day of school, I take my students on tours of the school. I simulate experiences, like going through the lunch line and making an appointment with the counselor, to ensure my students are comfortable navigating their new school environment. We must recognize the systems students must navigate within our schools and ensure they completely understand how to navigate them. When a system is an absolute barrier, we must then advocate to change that system. What systems in your school and district must students navigate and how can you help them do so?

As a teacher, I took the time to know my students, to meet their families, and then to be a vocal advocate for them. This seemingly tireless advocacy in reality only equated to 10 or 15 extra minutes each day to write a text, an email, have a conversation in the workroom, or run down to see the counselor for a few minutes. It wasn't time, it was commitment and follow through.

Also, everything we do requires a team. We cannot accomplish any of this without a dedicated group of people willing to place students above the system and to hold one another accountable at every turn.

We must observe our students. We must get to know them and we must listen to them. Sometimes that means questioning or adjusting protocols based on the needs of the students. We must challenge our own perceptions and those of our colleagues. We must listen to and respect one another and be there for one another. It is not the system that is important, it is the human beings, the students and the staff, who make up that system who are important.

Here is our call, educators. We must bring culture into our classrooms, both that of our students and of the English language. Culture shapes us and language is part of shaping culture.

Help students to confidently reach across differences by giving them experiences that challenge their perceptions and broaden their perspectives. Help them see the relevance of learning English and the relevance of language acquisition to their individual lives right now.

We must give students a voice and help them to see not only how language proficiency benefits them in achieving their goals, but also their potential impact on the world through language acquisition. Remember that kids will not automatically see language acquisition as an asset or as having an inherent value, we have to make it so.

Finally, the Coronavirus Pandemic will displace even more people across the globe and has already and will continue to exacerbate inequities in our school system. This is especially true for English Learners. Ensure that plans for instruction, whether face-to-face or via distance learning, consider the needs, the health and the safety of our English Learners.

We must give our students the tools and skills they need to be able to not only function but to make connections within their communities. Our end goal is English language proficiency, but more than that we want young people to be compassionate, to be empathetic, to be able to reach across differences, to believe in themselves and their abilities, and mostly to feel valued and welcome. We want young people to have hope.

We do this by recognizing that English language is a vehicle through which we help our students make connections and ensure they feel welcome and have a strong sense of belonging. This means facilitating connections with us as their educators. Connections between our students and their peers. Connections outside of our classrooms, our communities, our states and our nations. Connections that will help all of us move forward together, as global citizens of one world.